INSTITUTE OF PSYCHIATRY

Maudsley Monographs

THE DETECTION OF PSYCHIATRIC ILLNESS BY QUESTIONNAIRE

INSTITUTE OF PSYCHIATRY

MAUDSLEY MONOGRAPHS

Number Twenty-one

THE DETECTION OF PSYCHIATRIC ILLNESS BY QUESTIONNAIRE

A technique for the identification and assessment of non-psychotic psychiatric illness

By

DAVID P. GOLDBERG

M.A., D.M., M.R.C.P. (London & Edinburgh), D.P.M.

Senior Lecturer in Psychiatry
University of Manchester
Previously Lecturer in Psychiatry
Institute of Psychiatry

LONDON

OXFORD UNIVERSITY PRESS

NEW YORK   TORONTO

1972

Oxford University Press, Ely House, London W. 1

GLASGOW NEW YORK TORONTO MELBOURNE WELLINGTON
CAPE TOWN IBADAN NAIROBI DAR ES SALAAM LUSAKA ADDIS ABABA
DELHI BOMBAY CALCUTTA MADRAS KARACHI LAHORE DACCA
KUALA LUMPUR SINGAPORE HONG KONG TOKYO

ISBN 0 19 712143 8

© *Institute of Psychiatry 1972*

Printed in Great Britain
at the University Press, Oxford
by Vivian Ridler
Printer to the University

For my father

PAUL GOLDBERG, C.B.E.

*who did so much for the mentally
and physically disabled*

CONTENTS

LIST OF FIGURES

MAUDSLEY MONOGRAPHS

HENRY MAUDSLEY, from whom this series of monographs takes its name, was the founder of the Maudsley Hospital and the most prominent English psychiatrist of his generation. The Maudsley Hospital is now united with Bethlem Royal Hospital, and its medical school, renamed the Institute of Psychiatry, has become part of the British Postgraduate Medical Federation. It is entrusted by the University of London with the duty to advance psychiatry by teaching and research.

The monograph series reports work carried out in the Institute and in the associated Hospital. Some of the monographs are directly concerned with clinical problems; others, less obviously relevant, are in scientific fields that are cultivated for the furtherance of psychiatry.

Joint Editors

PROFESSOR SIR DENIS HILL
F.R.C.P., D.P.M.

PROFESSOR G. S. BRINDLEY
M.D., M.R.C.P., F.R.S.

with the assistance of

MISS S. E. HAGUE, B.Sc. (Econ.), M.A.

ACKNOWLEDGEMENTS

THIS research was carried out under the direction of Professor Michael Shepherd in the General Practice Research Unit of the Institute of Psychiatry, between 1965 and 1969, and was submitted as a thesis for the degree of Doctor of Medicine at the University of Oxford. It is a pleasure to record my debt of gratitude to Professor Shepherd, who has provided the facilities and a constant critical stimulus for the present research, and who has read the manuscript in draft and made detailed and helpful comments.

Dr. Barry Blackwell was a vigorous and enthusiastic collaborator in the General Practice validity study, which would have been much the poorer without his extensive research experience. Dr. Brian Creamer, gastro-enterologist at St. Thomas's Hospital, London, kindly allowed me to administer the questionnaire to his out-patients as part of a survey into psychiatric aspects of diseases of the small intestine that I was carrying out in his department. Dr. Karl Rickels and Dr. Peter Hesbacher of the Psycho-pharmacology Research Unit of the University of Pennsylvania provided me with the facilities and local know-how without which I could not have carried out the validation surveys in the United States. I am greatly indebted to Dr. D. Clark, Dr. W. Rial, Dr. H. Rosenfeld, Dr. A. Segal, and Dr. B Zamostein who allowed the validation surveys to be carried out in their private practices in Philadelphia.

I have been very fortunate in being able to consult Dr. A. E. Maxwell, Professor of Psychological Statistics at the Institute of Psychiatry, at all stages of the present work. Mr. Michael Clarke wrote the program for the discriminant function analysis, and supervised the analyses reported in CHAPTER III at the University of London's 'Atlas' Computer. Mr. Frank Gattoni of the London School of Economics transformed my requirements for the reliability and validity coefficients into a special Fortran program, and then supervised the numerous analyses reported in CHAPTER IV on the Atlas computer.

Workers in related fields have been kind enough to read drafts of the manuscripts and give me comments from their various standpoints. Dr. Alice Heim of the Psychological Laboratory, University of Cambridge, read the work at an early stage and made penetrating comments. My special thanks are due to both Dr. George Brown of the Department of Sociology, Bedford College, and Professor Henry Kedward of the University of Toronto, who have not only each made extremely helpful observations about the manuscript in draft but have been consistently sympathetic and encouraging about the work.

Miss Dorothy Rockett acted as a most efficient research assistant for the reliability and validity studies. I am indebted to the consultant staff of the Bethlem Royal and Maudsley Hospitals, of Cane Hill Hospital and St. John's

Hospital, Stone, for permission to give the questionnaire to their patients. My thanks are due to numerous colleagues at the Maudsley Hospital who made clinical ratings on their patients, to the registry staff and nurses who distributed the questionnaires, to Miss Pat Wills and the patients at the Day Hospital who coded and punched several thousand cards, and not least to the patients who have kindly filled in the questionnaire for me.

Finally, I would like to express my gratitude to my wife, who has read the manuscript with her usual care, and sustained me throughout the research.

Manchester   D. P. G.

1972

CHAPTER I

INTRODUCTION

PSYCHIATRIC illnesses may be divided into qualitative deviations from normal functioning, such as organic mental disorders and the functional psychoses, and quantitative deviations, such as neuroses and personality disorders. Epidemiological research has until comparatively recently concentrated on the predominantly psychotic illnesses, since patients in this group tend to receive in-patient treatment at some stage of their illnesses, and can therefore fairly easily be counted. (Malzberg, 1940; Ødegaard, 1946; Norris, 1959.) In the past 15 years psychiatric epidemiologists have begun to concentrate on attempts to measure the prevalence of non-psychotic illnesses in the community (Essen-Möller, 1956; Leighton, 1959; Srole, Langner, Michael, Opler, and Rennie, 1962; Hagnell, 1966), but as most patients with these conditions have not received hospital treatment, this has posed problems of identifying and defining the various disease entities as they exist in the population that has not come into contact with the psychiatric services. Since most patients with psychotic illnesses are known to the local psychiatric services (Ødegaard, 1952) and since the prevalence of psychotic illness is very small compared with the prevalence rates for all psychiatric illnesses, the identification of patients with non-psychotic psychiatric illnesses is a major problem in epidemiological research, since there is as yet no reliable screening test of acceptable validity.

The aim of the present study was to devise a self-administered questionnaire that would identify respondents with a non-psychotic psychiatric illness, by assessing the severity of their psychiatric disturbance. The questionnaire had to be easy to administer, acceptable to respondents, fairly short, and objective in the sense that it did not require the person distributing it to make subjective assessments about the respondent.

To say that a questionnaire will detect patients who are psychiatrically ill by assessing the severity of their psychiatric disturbance presupposes an axis of psychiatric disturbance on which any individual can be placed. It can be argued from available data (*vide supra*), as well as from clinical experience, that the distribution of psychiatric symptoms in the general population does not correspond to a sharp dichotomy between 'cases' and 'normals'. Psychiatric disturbance may be thought of as being evenly distributed throughout the population in varying degrees of severity, so that a more appropriate model might be that of an axis ranging from severe disorder to a hypothetical normality, with many steps between these end-points representing the various degrees of disturbance.

Having said this, it must be admitted that psychiatric illnesses are a heterogeneous collection of clinical syndromes and disease processes, and it seems
unlikely that there is any meaningful way of fitting them all on to the same
axis of severity of disturbance. However, the exclusion of the whole broad
category of organic mental disorders and the major functional psychoses from
the illnesses that the questionnaire is intended to detect will make the remaining range of illnesses less diverse.

There are strong practical as well as theoretical reasons for not attempting
to measure the whole range of psychiatric illnesses. It would be unrealistic to
attempt to detect conditions such as severe subnormality, senile dementia or
mania by a questionnaire since the nature of these conditions is such that most
patients would be unable to complete a questionnaire, and furthermore they
can be readily diagnosed on other grounds. An additional reason for excluding
conditions such as schizophrenia or the organic psychoses is that it is difficult
to devise a questionnaire which is at once short enough to be acceptable to a
large proportion of the population, and yet able to detect such a wide range
of psychiatric morbidity.

The illnesses that the questionnaire is intended to detect have been
described as 'non-psychotic' rather than 'neurotic' for a number of reasons.
Strictly speaking, the 'neuroses' refer to those illnesses enumerated under
Code 300 of the *International Classification of Diseases* (General Register
Office, 1968), and include relatively well-defined disease entities such as
obsessive compulsive neuroses, anxiety neuroses, and depressive neuroses.
Most psychiatrists would not include Code 301, the 'personality disorders',
as neuroses, yet many doctors seem to be referring to patients with personality
disorders when they speak of 'neurotics'. There is no general agreement about
whether to include Code 305, the 'physical disorders of presumably psycho-
genic origin', as neuroses, and it is fair to say that the term 'neurotic' has
come to be used in an imprecise way. The situation is further complicated
by the fact that clinical psychologists use the term 'neuroticism'—which they
frequently abbreviate to 'neurotic'—in a relatively precise yet different way
from the various medical usages referred to above. Eysenck (1947) uses the
term to refer to an aggregate of personality traits that are thought to remain
relatively stable in any individual over time. In contrast, the medical model
for neurotic illness is of a condition subject to relapses and remissions, with
great changes in severity over time. Since there is such a sharp contrast in
the way psychiatrists and psychologists use the word 'neurotic', and since even
among themselves doctors often use the term in an ill-defined way, it seemed
wiser to avoid it altogether in the present work.

To achieve its aim of detecting non-psychotic psychiatric illness at the time
it is completed, the questionnaire might reasonably deal with the way the
respondent has felt, thought and behaved in the time leading up to the
occasion on which it is completed. This means that the questionnaire should
give information only about the current mental state, so that a respondent

should score high if the questionnaire is completed during a period of illness, but low if it is completed during a period of health. The questionnaire will therefore neither be a measure of long-standing attributes of personality such as Eysenck's 'neuroticism', nor make assessments of the patient's liability to fall ill in the future. In its focus on the present at the expense of the past and the future, the questionnaire differs from most existing scales, which in the main aim to give information about their respondents which is fairly constant over time.

Non-psychotic Psychiatric Disorder as a Continuously Distributed Variable

If the model of a single axis ranging from normality to severe disturbance is accepted for the moment as a realistic working hypothesis, and if it proves possible to devise a questionnaire so that a given respondent is assigned a position on this axis according to known limits of error, an individual's score on the questionnaire could be thought of as a *quantitative estimate* of that individual's degree of psychiatric disturbance. There are indeed a number of uses for a measure that assigns an individual to a position on such an axis which do not depend on whether or not the individual is thought to be a 'case'.

First, it would be possible to compare the amount of psychiatric disturbance in two populations by a comparison of the means and standard deviations of scores in each population. Secondly, a given population could be tested on different occasions in order to follow the changes in psychiatric disturbance that occur with time. Finally, psychiatric disturbance as assessed by scores on the questionnaire could be correlated with other clinical and social variables in a given population.

Problems of Psychiatric Case Identification: Binomial Classification

If non-psychotic psychiatric disturbance is continuously distributed in a population, it follows that to ask what fraction of a population is psychiatrically disturbed is a meaningless question, since it presupposes that there is some answer to the problem of where normality ends and clinically significant disturbance begins.

It is, however, proper to ask what proportion of the population would be thought to have a clinically significant psychiatric disturbance if they were interviewed by a clinical psychiatrist, even though the value of such an assessment will in turn depend on the nature and reliability of the interview procedure that he uses. Blum (1962) in his discussion of this subject makes an important distinction between 'potential cases'—those picked out by questionnaires, key informants, and so on—and 'actual cases', by which he means those confirmed by psychiatric interview. The main value of a screening test in epidemiological research will be the first stage of what is essentially a two-stage process of case identification, the second stage being a full clinical interview by an experienced psychiatrist.

Even though there may be infinite gradations between psychological illness and normality, in most community surveys of psychiatric illness the investigator has to use a binomial classification, and to divide the population into 'cases' and 'normals'. It is notable that even those surveys that have started off with a quantitative model end by choosing some threshold point on their continuum that separates cases from normals, and so these surveys, too, can be reduced to a binomial model. To the extent that the questionnaire score gives an assessment of an individual's position on the proposed axis from normality to severe disturbance, it is therefore giving a *probability estimate* of the individual's being a psychiatric case.

These two uses of the questionnaire—as a method of assessing severity of disturbance and as a means of case identification—are of course interrelated, but the way in which the scores are used will be determined by the aims of any particular piece of research.

The present study, then, is an attempt to design a measuring instrument that will give an estimate of the degree of psychiatric disturbance of any individual without having to rely on the varying diagnostic standards of individual clinicians, and irrespective of whether the patient or anyone in his environment considers that he is ill.

In practice, as Blum wryly points out, it is the patient or those close to him who do the 'case identifying' in the community: the psychiatrist is but a final step. Moreover, as Felix and Bowers (1948) observe, the 'psychiatrist usually concurs with lay judgement and assigns a diagnostic tag in accordance with the formal patient role'.

CHAPTER II

REVIEW OF THE LITERATURE

THIS review of the literature will cover three loosely related areas. In the first section an account will be given of the more recent surveys of mental illness in the community, and these will be divided according to the method that was adopted for case identification. The case for some objective screening procedure for discovering potential cases having been argued, the next section will review the various self-administered questionnaires at present available, and state the reasons for devising a new questionnaire. The final section will set forth systematically the shortcomings of questionnaires.

1. *METHODS OF PSYCHIATRIC CASE IDENTIFICATION*

Even though the existence of psychiatric illness in the community was acknowledged early, not until the present century were statistical methods used to estimate the size of the problem. As will be seen in what follows, widely varying estimates of the prevalence of psychiatric illness have been provided by the numerous community surveys and general practice surveys reported to date. Many of these have relied on hospital records—so that an individual is counted as a case only if he has already been recognized as one— and this type of survey seems the least satisfactory from the point of view of trying to estimate the true prevalence of illness.

As Felix and Bowers (1948) point out: 'The researchers have no control over the case-finding process, over the record keeping, or even the diagnosis. Rather, they are dependent upon the public's uneven willingness to give up its mentally ill members and to support them in institutions, the hospital's unstandardized record-keeping activities, and the hospital staff's varied training and skill in classifying disorders.'

The objections to the use of hospital statistics become even greater if it is required to assess the prevalence of neurotic as well as psychotic illness. Thus, the next section will be concerned only with those surveys that have made direct approaches to a particular sample of the population and attempted to discover which of its members were or had been psychologically disturbed.

Interview by a Psychiatrist

In the absence of any objective criterion for what constitutes a psychiatric case, interview by an experienced psychiatrist becomes the ultimate method of case identification. There is no test of the validity of this procedure in the usual sense of that term, since if one psychiatrist's judgements are compared with those of another it becomes a test of reliability rather than validity.

In recent years increasing interest has been shown in the reliability of psychiatric diagnoses between psychiatrists (Kreitman, 1961; Norris, 1959; Schmidt and Fonda, 1956), and in his review of the field Foulds (1965) writes: 'The earlier and more pessimistic studies of the reliability of psychiatric diagnosis appear to have been superseded by better designed studies which suggest that inter-psychotic, neurotic and intra-psychotic reliabilities are satisfactorily high: whereas intra-neurotic reliabilities are low.' Reliability of psychiatric assessments between psychiatrists can be increased still further if standardized psychiatric interviews and rating-scales are used, and a number of these have been described in recent years (Goldberg, Cooper, Eastwood, Kedward, and Shepherd, 1970; Hetznecker, Gardner, Odoroff, and Turner, 1966; Kendell, Everitt, Cooper, Sartorius, and David, 1968; Overall and Gorham, 1962; Spitzer, Fleiss, Burdock, and Hardesty, 1964).

If interview by a psychiatrist is used as the method of case identification in community surveys, the reliability of the procedure can be made much higher if steps are taken to control interviewer error, if the terms used in the surveys are carefully defined, if a pilot study is carried out, and if some standardized interview procedure is adopted. It must be admitted, however, that relatively few surveys have been carried out which depend on psychiatrists as the sole case identifiers.

An early field survey was carried out by Clouston (1911) when he studied the family histories of 83 families in a single parish in one of the Orkney Islands. He gives no details of his interview technique, and reports, 'I made no selection, but where the family and its history were unknown to me I omitted it'. This last observation reduced the significance of his main findings, but his survey is notable for having included 'cases of mild weakness of mind, and mild attacks of depression of mind, neither of which would have been counted as unsoundness of mind at all by an unscientific observer'. He found mental cases in 41 of his 83 families, with multiple cases in most of the 41 families with abnormal members.

The study that best illustrates the method of using psychiatrists as the sole case identifiers is that started by Essen-Möller (1956) at Lund, and carried on by Hagnell (1959, 1968). Two adjoining parishes with a total of 2500 inhabitants in a rural area in the south of Sweden were intensively studied by Essen-Möller and three colleagues in the summer of 1947. There was no sampling procedure; every member of the population was approached and interviewed by a psychiatrist. The interview was relatively unstructured, but since the interviewer aimed to collect information in a number of specified areas at some point in the course of the interview it would count as a 'guided interview'. There was no formal substudy to measure the inter-rater reliability of the procedure.

Essen-Möller did not divide his population into 'cases' and 'normals' but arranged individuals on a continuum ranging from definite mental illness through abnormalities of personality to complete normality. He found a lifetime prevalence of 1·7 per cent for psychosis, 5·17 per cent for neuroses, and 0·98 per cent for oligophrenia. A large proportion of the population were thought to be personality variants, and only 39·6 per cent of men and 32·8 per cent of women were thought to be normal.

Hagnell (1959, 1968) revisited these patients and found it possible to ask questions that were much more overtly psychiatric in content than Essen-Möller had thought it prudent to use. This procedure resulted in higher figures for neurosis and oligophrenia, although the figure for psychosis remained about the same (psychosis, 1·7 per cent; neurosis, 13·1 per cent; and mental deficiency, 1·2 per cent). In assessing the rates for neurosis Hagnell aimed to exclude minor disturbances: 'I have included only the conditions which are acute, defined and pronounced as to symptoms and onset. They must also indicate a disease or a deviation from the patient's usual physical capability and capacity for work.'

The term 'lifetime prevalence' refers in his study to the risk of developing mental illness up to the present age of the subjects. Hagnell also computed the 'cumulated risk' for developing a mental illness, and, in the 10-year period of his survey, showed that this is 11·3 per cent for men and 20·4 per cent for women, whereas the estimated cumulated risk up to the age of 60 is 43·4 per cent for men and 73·0 per cent for women. However, of these only 7·9 per cent of men and 15·4 per cent of women risk contracting a mental illness causing 'severe impairment' of function.

It is surprising that so few investigators have used a procedure whereby screening instruments—questionnaires and key informants—suggest potential cases and actual psychiatric cases are then identified by psychiatric interview. Lin (1953) used this technique in a prevalence survey of mental illness in Formosa, but although his figures for psychoses were comparable to those of other investigators his figure of 1·2 cases per 1000 population for neurotic illness suggests that his informants did not report many potential cases.

In some surveys psychiatrists have interviewed some individuals but have left other interviews to trained research assistants or to social workers. Eaton and Weil's study (1955) of mental disorder among the Hutterites involved a total of 2000 interviews. Of these, the psychiatrist interviewed nearly 300 patients, but the majority of those classed as mentally disturbed were interviewed not by him, but by a team of six research assistants acting on information given by key informants. This study suggested a prevalence of only 16·7 per 1000.

In Cole, Branch, and Shaw's (1957) survey at Salt Lake City, the interviews were carried out by a third-year psychiatric resident and a PSW both supervised by a psychiatrist. Little information is given about interview technique, except that the interview was unstructured and psychiatric questions were asked towards the end. Twenty-five families were interviewed in each of eight separate city blocks. The authors accepted information about absent family members from their informant in each family, and arrived at a prevalence rate of 333 per 1000 for all mental disorders in people over the age of 16. It seems likely that their criteria for what constituted a psychiatric case were radically different from those of Eaton and Weil.

Case Identification by Research Assistants

In most community surveys of mental illness the psychiatrist has evaluated the notes of an interview carried out by another person rather than interviewed the patient himself. Some have used non-psychiatric medical colleagues to interview the patient; others have trained research assistants to administer a standardized interview.

The survey carried out at Baltimore by Pasamanick, Roberts, Lemkau, and Krueger (1959) is an example of the first method. The patients were seen by physicians at the Johns Hopkins Hospital for a full medical assessment. If the physician made any mention of mental disorder in his assessment, the notes were examined by a psychiatrist. For one-third of the patients for whom the examining physician recorded a psychiatric diagnosis this diagnosis was deleted by the psychiatrist. There is no mention of the reverse process, presumably because the research design makes it unlikely. The result of the survey was that in the non-institutionalized population the rate for 'obvious mental illness' was 93·4 per 1000.

When non-medical interviewers are used, it is usual to structure the interview in some way in order to increase the reliability of the ratings. If the interviewer is free to ask questions in ways which seem most appropriate, and free to ask any 'probe' questions that may seem indicated, it is called a 'guided interview', while if the interviewer has to stick rigidly to some prearranged format it is called a 'structured interview'.

One of the earliest surveys of mental illness in the community was carried out by Rosanoff (1927) in Nassau County, New York. Each person referred for suspected mental abnormality was interviewed by a member of a team of 15 female research assistants, and final decisions as to what constituted a case were made by a physician with extensive psychiatric training. They found a prevalence rate of 36·5 per 1000 for all mental disorders.

In the Williamson County Survey Roth and Luton (1943) attempted to estimate the number of people who should be under psychiatric care at any particular point in time in Tennessee. They used two social workers and a psychiatric nurse as their interviewers, and used persons referred by key informants. They arrived at a figure of 46·7 per 1000 for all disorders active on the census day.

The best example of the use of the 'guided' interview in case identification is Gruenberg's (1954, 1959) Syracuse Survey, in which intensively trained interviewers were allowed a good deal of freedom to ask their questions as seemed appropriate to them, and the results were then read by a panel of three professionals, only one of whom was a psychiatrist. This study is notable for the fact that some awareness was displayed about the possible limitations of the screening method, and the psychiatrist reinterviewed a small proportion of the population. It was found that the guided interview had tended to underestimate the prevalence of psychiatric illness.

More recently, two large surveys of mental illness have used highly structured interviews administered by research assistants and have produced prevalence rates for mental illness much higher than any previously reported. Srole and his associates' (1962) Midtown Manhattan Survey used trained interviewers to administer a very long, highly structured interview that took from 2 to 4 hours to complete. Standardization, and therefore reliability, were achieved at the cost of spontaneity of response. Interviewers were allowed to note down any spontaneous remarks made by their subjects, as well as any abnormalities of manner and behaviour. The completed schedules were independently rated by two psychiatrists, whose respective ratings over the 1660 subjects correlated with one another $+0.75$ on a seven-point scale of severity of disturbance. This survey found that no fewer than 815 per 1000 had symptoms of some sort, and that 234 per 1000 were 'impaired' by their symptoms and would count as psychiatric cases. The authors considered, but rejected, the hypothesis that their sample might contain more than its fair share of cases, and did not consider that their notion of a psychiatric case was too inclusive.

Their figures are supported by those found in the Stirling County Survey by Leighton, Harding, Macklin, Macmillan, and Leighton (1963). Trained research assistants administered a long structured interview that included the Health Opinion Survey, which will be described more fully below. The interviewers were allowed to make their own observations about the respondents' manner. The completed schedule was assessed by a series of psychiatrists who also saw impressions from two other physicians and at least one other community source, and any relevant hospital or institutional records. Four raters were used, who eventually made 'joint evaluations' about each case. The two main substudies were called the 'Family Life Survey' and the 'Bristol Health Survey'.

The Family Life Survey consisted of 1010 interviews of heads of households or their wives taken from the whole of Stirling County. This gave a prevalence rate of 577 per 1000 population who were 'genuine psychiatric cases'. The Bristol Health Survey consisted of only 140 interviews with a representative sample of all persons over the age of 18 in the town of Bristol. The authors note that more questions were asked about health in this substudy, and the quality of the interviewing was better. It produced the astonishing figure of 690 per 1000 'genuine psychiatric cases'. Even if one takes the figures for 'genuine psychiatric cases with impairment of function', the prevalence rate is still 420 per 1000 population.

These results are so much at variance with everyday experience that one is entitled to look for some other explanation of them.

One possible explanation is that the results are in some way an artefact of

the experimental method used by the investigators. In favour of this explanation would be Leighton and his associates' observation that 'the attempt to
make a diagnosis in the usual clinical sense must be abandoned' (Leighton,
Harding, Macklin, Macmillan, and Leighton, 1963, p. 48). Examples of the
protocols are given in appendices to both the Midtown Manhattan and the
Stirling County Surveys, and it is difficult to get a clear idea of the person
being described from reading a disconnected series of responses to questionnaire items on a disembodied form. It seems to be a denial of the usual
diagnostic process. To an outsider it seems odd that neither group of investigators carried out a series of blind clinical assessments on a subsample of their
population, as Gruenberg did at Syracuse.

Another possibility is that the criteria for what constitutes a psychiatric case
differ radically in Europe and the United States. Hagnell and Leighton (1969)
carried out joint evaluations on 139 patients from the Stirling County Survey
and 213 patients from the Lund Survey. Using Leighton's criteria for
neurosis, Hagnell's figures for neurosis rise from 13·1 per cent to 35–40 per
cent, and for mental deficiency rise from 1·2 per cent to 10 per cent, while the
figures for psychosis do not alter. The difference between the two surveys
is still significant, but it can be seen that the greater part of the apparent
difference is due to differing thresholds for case identification.

Case Identification by Validated, Structured Interview or Test

The standardized interviews described so far resemble one another in that
after they have been completed each subject's replies must be assessed by an
expert or a panel of experts. An alternative procedure is to design the interview in such a way that the person administering it can compute a score
which indicates whether the respondent is likely to be a psychiatric case. In
order to do this the structured interview would need to be subjected to at
least a validity study, where the score generated by the structured interview
is compared with the results of a blind, independent, clinical assessment.

Although a great number of structured clinical interviews and rating-scales
are now available for use with identified psychiatric patients (see Lorr, 1960;
Hamilton, 1959, 1960; and Kendell, Everitt, Cooper, Sartorius, and David,
1968) comparatively few can be administered by a non-psychiatrist and used
as a method of case identification.

The 'Health Opinion Survey'. Macmillan's (1959) Health Opinion Survey
(HOS) consists of 75 'health orientated' queries, scored 'often-sometimes-
never' and derived from the United States Army Neuropsychiatric Screening
Test. A complex scoring process used weighted scores for each item derived
from a discriminant function analysis. The calibration study used as 'normals'
those respondents who came from farms that had been designated 'good
farms' by the County Agricultural Agent, while the 'cases' were inmates at
local mental hospitals. The content of the items has a heavy somatic bias, and
the method of identifying normals seems open to question.

In a validation study 64 respondents were each given a 30-minute interview by a psychiatrist. The results are complex, since not only the psychiatrist but also the questionnaire were allowed to classify subjects as 'doubtful'. These results are shown as TABLE I to allow comparison with the validity survey of the present questionnaire.

TABLE 1

CLINICAL ASSESSMENT BY PSYCHIATRIST COMPARED WITH SCORES
ON THE HOS FOR 64 SUBJECTS

(*After Macmillan, 1959*)

PREDICTION BY	CLASSIFICATION BY PSYCHIATRIST		
HOS	*Well*	*Doubtful*	*Sick*
Sick	3	16	10
Doubtful	4	1	2
Well	22	6	0
Totals	*29*	*23*	*12*

The author interprets these results as showing only a 14 per cent discrepancy between the results of his questionnaire and his clinical assessment. This surprising figure is arrived at by considering only those subjects that could be confidently categorized as 'well' or 'sick'. The procedure of excluding from consideration the very cases about which difficulty may arise makes these results much less impressive from the point of view of case identification.

This same study is reported at greater length by Leighton and his associates (1963, pp. 220–33). From this account the test-retest correlation coefficient for the 64 subjects was +0·87, but unfortunately the time between the tests is not stated. The correlation between the HOS score and the authors' various assessments of severity of psychiatric disturbance is only +0·5, and they conclude that 'it follows from this that no reasonably valid prediction can be made of whether a particular individual is a "case" or not'. They also add that there is no significant difference between the mean HOS scores of adjacent groups of patients, when the groups are arranged in order of ascending severity.

Langner's 22-item Screening Test. Langner's test is administered as a structured interview, and consists of the 22 items drawn from the entire pool of psychiatric items used in the Midtown Manhattan Survey that discriminated between two criterion groups of respondents. These were 72 'known well' respondents chosen on the basis of a half-hour interview with a psychiatrist from a 'larger group', and 139 'known ill' respondents who were currently receiving psychiatric treatment. Each item was shown to correlate well with the rating psychiatrists' overall judgement of mental health over the 1660 interviews that are the basis of the Midtown Survey itself. The items came mainly from the MMPI and the United States Army's Neuropsychiatric Screening Adjunct, and are heterogeneous. Nine of the 22 items are current symptoms such as, 'There seems to be a fullness (clogging) in my nose much of the time'; a further 3 are personality traits such as, 'Are you the worrying type?'; the remaining 10 are questions about past history such as 'Have you ever been bothered with shortness of breath?'. One would expect the effect of this to be to generate a score that is relatively stable over time for a given respondent rather than to explore the current mental state.

When the test is used for screening Langner (1962) showed that the best threshold to adopt was between 3 and 4, and he demonstrated the effectiveness of this both in detecting illness among the 40 Midtown respondents who were currently found to be receiving psychiatric treatment, and among the entire population of 1660 respondents by comparing the screening score against the psychiatrists' mental health rating. In the former group the screening test misses 40 per cent of the patients (i.e. a sensitivity of 60 per cent), although it does slightly less badly with the larger group.

TABLE 2

A COMPARISON OF SCORE ON LANGNER'S 22-ITEM SCREENING TEST WITH THE OVERALL MENTAL HEALTH RATING FOR THE 1660 RESPONDENTS INTERVIEWED ON THE MIDTOWN SURVEY

(After Langner, 1962)

SCORE ON 22-ITEM SCREENING TEST	OVERALL MENTAL HEALTH RATING	
	Unimpaired	*Impaired*
Probable cases (score 4+)	232	286
Probable normals (score 0–3)	1039	103
Totals	*1271*	*389*

This table generates the following values:

    Specificity (proportion of normals with low scores) = 81·7%
    Sensitivity (proportion of cases with high scores) = 73·5%
    Overall misclassification rate   = 20·2%

The overall misclassification rate is obtained by expressing the number of cases incorrectly classified by the screening test as a percentage of the total number of patients screened. The terms 'specificity' and 'sensitivity' are discussed by Reid (1960) and Wilson and Jungner (1968).

These results are doubly disappointing when it is recalled that the screening score and the mental health rating are in no sense independent measures, since the latter is partly based on the former.

Manis, Brawer, Hunt, and Kercher (1963) attempted to validate the instrument, but found that the scale failed to measure the relative positions of individuals on the scale, and could only be thought of as differentiating between the average health of groups. Even the scale's ability to differentiate between 'known groups' of patients was not entirely satisfactory, since the authors tested the hypothesis that when the mean scores of groups were compared, patients in an admission ward would score higher than those in a predischarge ward, and these in turn would be higher than those found in various community groups. In fact, patients in the predischarge wards had lower mean scores than two of the community groups examined. The authors conclude: 'Improved survey techniques need to be constructed and validated. Until such instruments are available, the present scales offer a preliminary, if crude, measure of *group* mental health.'

In an interesting subsequent paper, Brawer, Hunt, and Kercher (1964) showed that when the screening test is used on a random sample from an urban–rural community (Kalamazoo County, Mich.) the rate of probable cases per 1000 population is identical to that found in Midtown Manhattan, even though only half as many patients are being treated by psychiatrists.

Beck's Depression Inventory. A rather different approach is represented by the Beck Depression Inventory, a short standardized series of questions aimed at detecting depression and administered by a skilled worker. Paradoxically, when the scale was administered to non-psychiatric populations, Schwab, Bialow, Clemmons, Martin, and Holzer (1967) observed that patients with high scores tended to receive diagnoses other than depression, but they did not say what these diagnoses were. The scale is described by Beck, Ward, Mendelson, Mock, and Erbaugh (1961) and consists of 21 questions concerned with depression. The subject must choose the answer that most nearly describes himself from a number of possible responses. The scale had a satisfactory reliability, and the validity was assessed by comparing the scores of 409 patients with independent assessments of depth of depression by experienced psychiatrists. These assessments were compressed into two categories for the purposes of statistical treatment: 'no depression' was combined with 'mild depression', and 'moderate depression' was combined with 'severe depression'; Pearson's biserial correlation coefficient was then found to be approximately $+0.66$.

The authors went on to consider the percentage of misclassifications produced by the questionnaire by examining 'non-adjacent' clinical categories. They divided the 409 patients into four clinical groups—no depression, mild, moderate and severe depression—and compared 'no depression' with 'moderate depression' ignoring the patients with 'mild depression'. Even so 23 per cent of their patients were misclassified. (It will be recalled that Macmillan did this with the results of his validation study of the Health Opinion Survey, and there would seem to be as little warrant for it in the one study as in the other.)

Schwab, Bialow, Clemmons, Martin, and Holzer (1967) carried out a validation study of the Beck Depression Inventory on 153 medical in-patients, by correlating their scores with the results of a standardized psychiatric interview using the Hamilton Scale. Forty-four per cent of their patients had supra-threshold scores, and the correlation between the Inventory score and the Hamilton Scale score was +0·75. In a small validation study on 37 patients in England (Metcalfe and Goldman, 1965) the psychiatrist assigned patients to the four categories used by Beck and his associates, and the authors computed a correlation coefficient using Kendall's rank order coefficient 'tau', which they computed was +0·62. They found that 14 per cent of their patients were misclassified by the Inventory, but unfortunately followed Beck and his associates in ignoring the 'mildly depressed' group. When they ignored the 'moderately depressed' group and compared the 'mildly depressed' with the 'severely depressed' they found that 21 per cent were misclassified by the Inventory.

The Symptom Rating Test. Kellner (1967) and Kellner and Sheffield (1967) describe a semistructured interview designed to assess changes in symptoms in non-psychotic patients. The patient is verbally presented with a checklist of symptoms, and has then to make a series of self-ratings dealing with the intensity, frequency, and duration of most of the symptoms on a set of five-point scales. The interview is called the 'symptom rating-scale', and has been designed to assess change in patients undergoing treatment rather than for case identification. It has recently become available in a self-administered version, which will be discussed in the next section.

Two further scales have been designed by clinical psychologists in this country. Ingham (1965) has adapted Shapiro's (1961) 'Personal Questionnaire' for case identification in epidemiology, and Foulds (1965) has described his 'Symptom–Sign Inventory'.

The Personal Questionnaire. Ingham's work has the advantage of almost completely eliminating many of the shortcomings associated with less sophisticated questionnaires, but his method has some limitations: the number of symptoms that can be explored on any occasion is necessarily limited, and the test must be administered by an experienced clinical psychologist. The scoring procedure is complex, and in the pilot study reported above no fewer than 23 per cent of Ingham's respondents refused to co-operate with him.

The Symptom–Sign Inventory. Foulds's (1965) Symptom–Sign Inventory (SSI) consists of 80 questions which are administered by an interviewer and scored 'yes' or 'no'. Foulds has pointed out that most personality scales and complaint inventories fail to distinguish between personality traits and symptoms. Traits are ego-syntonic and of relatively long duration, whereas signs and symptoms are relatively rare, are distressing and signify a break in the normal continuity of behaviour. If information is being sought about relatively enduring attributes of personality such as 'neuroticism', 'extroversion', or 'hysteroid personality', then it is essential that the test should consist of items that reflect *traits* of personality. If, on the other hand, information is being sought either of a diagnostic nature or about the severity of illness, then the test should consist of the *symptoms and signs of illness*.

This is an important and fundamental criticism of existing scales, since, for example, the 'neuroticism' scale of the Maudsley Personality Inventory (MPI) contains some items which are really symptoms, and the Cornell Medical Inventory contains many items which are traits. In this connection it is interesting to note that Ingham (1966) has shown that the 'neuroticism' scores of the MPI become lower in patients who improve most after a psychiatric illness, when remeasured 3 years later at follow-up. If the measuring scale were not contaminated with symptoms, this would probably not occur to the same extent. However, Kendell and DiScipio (1968) have shown that if depressed patients are asked to disregard their illness and to fill in the MPI as they would 'when you are your usual self', then they obtain significantly lower 'N' scores than they would otherwise have done.

The SSI was designed not as a method of case identification in epidemiology, but as a diagnostic instrument. It can, however, be used as a method of case identification, and when tested on 263 psychiatrically ill, and 73 apparently well, subjects achieved a fairly good discrimination. Using a threshold score of 4 or more to indicate illness, and 3 or less to indicate health, 89 per cent of the clinically ill group and 86 per cent of the apparently normal group were correctly placed.

Foulds and Hope (1968) have identified 20 items in the SSI which they refer to as a 'personal disturbance scale', since it has been shown to discriminate between a group of 69 'normal women' and their calibration groups of psychiatric patients. Although the authors envisage that the scale might be used as a screening device in epidemiological and social surveys, they properly emphasize that their standardization data were obtained when the 20 items of the 'personal disturbance scale' were given as part of the full-length SSI, as an interview administered by a clinical psychologist. The authors do not state their criteria of normality for the 69 'normal women', nor why it was not thought necessary to give the scale to 'normal men'. If the scale is to be used in epidemiological surveys, it would be interesting to see the results of a validity study where a population of patients with a proportion of abnormal members received the personal disturbance scale and an independent psychiatric assessment, but such a study has not so far been reported.

The SSI would appear to be an instrument of acceptable validity, and is indeed in many ways comparable to the present questionnaire. Each instrument has its own advantage and limitations, and consideration of these will indicate which should be chosen for any particular research design.

The SSI provides diagnostic information in addition to the information about severity from the total score, and since it is administered by a skilled interviewer it is both possible to make some subjective assessments of the respondent and to persuade reluctant or illiterate subjects to become respondents. On the other hand, since it is administered by an interviewer it is at once less convenient and more expensive as a community research tool, and is also subject to 'interviewer errors' and 'yea-saying bias', which will be discussed in a later section.

Case Identification by General Practitioners

The earliest psychiatric survey by a general practitioner was by Johan Bremer (1951) who reported on an isolated community of 1000 persons in northern Norway, throughout the last war. Bremer had close personal knowledge of his practice and stated that there was hardly a person who had not consulted him; he had been in every house and knew of every case of illness: 'I knew the inhabitants at very close quarters, knew their joys and, in particular, their sorrows and worries.' Perhaps because of this, Bremer estimated that no fewer than 25 per cent of the population were 'psychic exceptionals'—an opinion that he expressed only after he had carried out what was in effect a psychiatric interview in order to establish the subject as a case.

Since then many more studies have been reported with very varying results: Kellner (1963) reviews no fewer than 25 surveys in Britain alone, with widely varying consultation and prevalence rates from one survey to another. Shepherd and his associates' (1966) survey of psychiatric morbidity in 46 London general practices found that individual doctors varied in their estimates of psychiatric morbidity from as few as 37·8 to as many as 323 per 1000 patients at risk. To some extent, the authors realized that true differences in prevalence from one practice to another might account for this ninefold difference, but they demonstrate that observer factors are also important determinants of the interpractice variation.

As far as the lone surveys are concerned, the doctors who undertake them are inevitably self-selected, and this fact alone is likely to influence the reported prevalence rates: for example, a doctor interested in psychotherapy may attract a larger number of neurotic patients to his practice than one who is hostile to emotionally disturbed patients. Furthermore, not only varying diagnostic standards but also varying classifications will account for much more variation—a point made by Kessel (1960). In addition, morbidity may be measured in different ways, so that the various sorts of prevalence and consultation rates are confused, and the populations in which the prevalence rates are computed in any case may not be demographically similar. Standards of recording vary with the motivation and work-load of the individual investigator, and if extra workers are enlisted to help with the analysis of data the sources of error increase still further.

It is thus clear that although general practice is a rich potential source of information about neurotic illness in the community, there is a pressing need for a research instrument to assess psychiatric morbidity irrespective of the differing standards of observers, and this was indeed the starting-point for the present research.

General practitioners may be used as important key informants in a particular form of community survey carried out by a psychiatrist. In this method a cohort of patients, who were about 60 years of age, are followed by an exhaustive search of all public records. The research psychiatrist discusses each patient in detail with his general practitioner, who therefore becomes the single most important case identifier of minor psychiatric illness. This method was originated by Klemperer (1933) in Munich, and was used both by Freming (1951) for his survey on Bornholm, and by Helgason (1964) for his survey of psychiatric illness in Iceland. An obvious limitation of the method, not mentioned by any of these authors, is that most general practitioners who were alive during the early years of the lives of the patients who make up the cohort will necessarily be dead and so unavailable for interview at the time of the survey, which must produce a loss of information. The prevalence figures for psychosis, where the investigator leans far more heavily on mental hospital records, would be expected not to show this effect. Indeed, in Bornholm the psychotics outnumbered the neurotics by almost 2:1.

The method has been little used outside Scandinavia, although Jones's (1962) study of mental disorder in Anglesey was similar in some respects. In this 1-year period prevalence study of mental disorder the research psychiatrist visited every general practitioner in Anglesey and went over their entire collection of case cards with them. It produced a prevalence for all psychiatric disorders of between 3 per cent and 4 per cent.

The prevalence figures for neurotic illness found by these more systematic methods using general practitioners as case identifiers have generally been much lower than those found by direct interview methods in the major surveys already reviewed. A clue to the reason for this disparity is provided by the following quotations.

Jones writes of his Anglesey study that minor mental illness was 'virtually a normal thing, once passed was rapidly forgotten. Even when a general practitioner remembered such an episode he would generally only mention it in passing and would not regard the patient as "psychiatric".'

Taylor (1954) visited 30 English general practices to gather material for a book that he was writing entitled *Good General Practice*. The following quotation is revealing: 'I was surprised to find during the survey how comparatively seldom the good general practitioner diagnoses neurotic illness. Patients with organic illness react with a measure of anxiety which can be mistaken for neurosis.'

Both these authors are psychiatrists, yet they, and presumably many of the general practitioners with whom they worked, seem to regard neurotic illness as something chronic. Although they clearly recognize that minor affective illness is common and often transient, the fact that they do not count such illnesses as 'neuroses' may account for some of the discrepancy referred to above.

2. SELF-ADMINISTERED QUESTIONNAIRES AS SCREENING TESTS

The wide differences in prevalence rates reported in the various community surveys are due in large part to differences in the method used for case identification. The ultimate method of case identification must remain interview by an experienced psychiatrist, and the introduction of various rating and scoring procedures can greatly increase the reliability of this procedure.

It has been shown that if psychiatrists rate a schedule that has been completed by a research assistant the procedure is unreal and results in very high reported rates. On the other hand, if general practitioners or other 'key informants' are used as case identifiers one is necessarily limited by each informant's notion of what constitutes a case—and one cannot possibly learn about cases that the key informants do not know about themselves—so that it is probable that this procedure results in under-reporting of cases.

Since it is usually impracticable for a psychiatrist to interview each member of a population, a standardized screening instrument of known reliability and validity is clearly desirable.

The advantages of using self-administered questionnaires to identify cases are fairly self-evident. Large numbers of subjects can be approached, the method is relatively cheap and is not as time-consuming as most interview methods. There are no problems of varying standards between different interviewers, and most of the questionnaires are objective in that the person scoring them does not have to make subjective judgements.

The most common type of questionnaire is the 'complaint inventory', basically a list of symptoms but often with some personality traits included. In most the respondent is expected to mark 'yes' against those symptoms or traits that he has, and in some others he marks as 'true' propositions that he thinks apply to him.

Gurin, Veroff, and Feld (1960), while praising the simplicity and acknowledging the face validity of symptom lists, point out that 'the lack of a developed conceptual and theoretical framework for this technique limits its appeal'. Cartwright (1959) has shown that the wording of the questions, the time-span asked about, and the categories used in coding, all affect the reported morbidity rates. Blum (1962) has also objected to a direct count of symptoms on the grounds that it constitutes a 'tabulation of misery' and may result in too high a rate of case identification. He points out that this will be especially true for individuals of low social class, since miseries and dissatisfaction are universally found in people of low status in industrial societies. In this connection it is interesting that Shepherd, Cooper, Brown, and Kalton (1966) in their General Practice Survey found that the M–R score of the Cornell Medical Inventory was significantly higher in low social groups for both sexes (Shepherd, Cooper, Brown, and Kalton, 1966, p. 120).

Many of these objections will be met if the questionnaire is carefully calibrated on a sample of the population on which it will eventually be used, and if an item analysis is carried out, with only those items selected for the final questionnaire which discriminate between calibration groups that have been carefully matched for social class. Unfortunately, very few of the self-administered questionnaires to be described here appear to have done this.

Some of the existing inventories and scales that could be used for psychiatric case identification will now be described. No mention will be made of the many questionnaires that are intended to measure personality; questionnaires intended to generate diagnostic information will be mentioned only if they would also be suitable for case identification.

The Cornell Medical Inventory (CMI)

The CMI was originally designed to screen recruits in the Second World War and was intended both to save doctors' time and to increase the accuracy of clinical diagnosis. The present version was described by Brodman, Erdman, Lorge, Wolff, and Broadbent in 1949, revised in 1956, and found to be of particular use in identifying emotional disturbance: apparently 'normal' people who had high scores turned out to be emotionally disturbed at subsequent psychiatric interview (Brodman, Erdman, Lorge, Wolff, and Broadbent, 1952a). It is easy to administer, and unskilled interpreters may make psychiatric assessments on the basis of CMI scores which are as good as those of skilled interpreters. Brodman, Erdman, Lorge, Wolff, and Broadbent (1949) replied to the objection that patients might give dishonest replies to the questionnaire by showing that patients answer questions on thc CMI as honestly as they do to the physician's oral interview.

The CMI has been used as a method of psychiatric case identification in many situations and countries. It has bccn used in general hospital practice by Brodman et al. (1952b), Erdman (1952), Culpan, Davies, and Oppenheim (1960), and Richman, Slade, and Gordon (1966). In most of these studies fairly high numbers of potential cases have been identified in all departments, dependent upon the threshold score adopted and the country in which the survey took place.

In a community study Brodman et al. (1952a) showed an incidence of potential cases of 10 per cent for men and 30 per cent for women from the random New York 'normal' population, and a figure of 52 per cent for men and 65 per cent for women from a population of known neurotics in a New York Hospital. Clearly, a questionnaire that misses about 40 per cent of a population of known psychiatric cases can hardly be used as a confident means of case identification.

Abrahamson, Terepolsky, Brook, and Kark (1965) administered the CMI to a random group from a Jerusalem housing project. Although the CMI was found to have little or no value in indicating specific disturbances, it correlated well with ratings made currently by physicians of the respondents' overall and emotional health. The physicians rated emotional health on a four-point scale ranging from '1: Appears quite well, disturbance minimal' to '4: Emotionally disturbed, definitely needs help'. An item analysis of the CMI was then performed using only Groups 1 and 4 as calibration groups— Groups 2 and 3 being ignored. Thirteen questions were found which were at least 10 times more likely to be answered 'yes' by an emotionally ill person than by an emotionally well person, and these were designated the 'key questions'.

A number of workers in this country have used the CMI to identify psychiatric cases in general practice. Herst (1965) persuaded 88 per cent of all patients in his practice over the age of 15 to fill in the CMI, and at the same time made his own independent assessment of each patient's psychiatric state on his own 'subjective scale'. Considering the congruence of the two assessments, he writes of the CMI scores that 'at each cut off level a proportion was misdiagnosed, although the number of "normals" diminishes at each higher score'.

Brown and Fry (1962) reported on the CMI scores of three subgroups within Fry's general practice. A probability sample of consecutive attenders was divided into two groups, 30 with 'neurosis' and 140 with other diagnoses. It was found that only 57 per cent of the patients with 'neurosis' would have been identified as cases by the questionnaire, whereas 19 per cent of those patients with other diagnoses would have been 'misclassified', since they had supra-threshold scores. In a substudy the psychiatrist interviewed 32 cases chosen by the general practitioner from his whole list as examples of 'neurosis'. All these were confirmed as severe neurotics by the psychiatrist on interview, yet only 84 per cent of this group would have been identified by their high CMI scores.

Rawnsley (1966) used his own modification of the CMI to compare the assessments made by the CMI with his own independent psychiatric assessments of 76 members of a random sample of a rural population in the Vale of Glamorgan. His modification consisted of using only 100 of the original items, and having each question typed out on a separate card. The patient then had to sort the cards into two piles for 'yes' and 'no'. This test was administered by research workers and at psychiatric assessment a few days later the patient was classified as healthy, physically ill, or as a psychiatric case on the basis of an unstructured interview. This is one of the few studies where a population containing only a proportion of psychiatric cases was given a questionnaire as well as an independent assessment by a psychiatrist, so making it possible to assess the value of this modification of the CMI as a screening instrument.

Rawnsley (1969) has very kindly made the raw results of this study available to the author. In the analysis which follows, his 'physically ill' patients have been combined with his 'healthy' patients and called 'normals', in order to facilitate the comparison between psychiatric normals and psychiatric cases. Since there is no agreed threshold score to distinguish between cases and normals for this version of the CMI, a number of different 'cutting scores' were tried out, of which only three are shown in TABLE 3.

It can be seen from the table that the best discrimination between cases and normals is achieved by adopting a threshold of 15 symptoms, and that this is associated with an overall misclassification of 18·4 per cent. In practice such a threshold would not be seriously considered since it results in missing almost a third of the cases, and although this low sensitivity can be improved by lowering the threshold score, the number of normals incorrectly identified as cases—the specificity—becomes unsatisfactory, and the overall misclassification rises to 28·6 per cent.

TABLE 3

THE EFFECTS OF ADOPTING DIFFERENT CUTTING SCORES WITH RAWNSLEY'S ADAPTATION OF THE CMI IN THE SCREENING OF PSYCHIATRIC PATIENTS IN THE VALE OF GLAMORGAN

CUTTING SCORE	SENSITIVITY *True positives* / *Total number of cases* %	SPECIFICITY *True negatives* / *Total number of normals* %	OVERALL MISCLASSIFICATION RATE %
15/14	70·6 (12/17)	84·7 (50/59)	18·4
13/12	76·4 (13/17)	79·6 (47/59)	21·0
10/9	100 (17/17)	64·4 (38/59)	28·6

Shepherd, Cooper, Brown, and Kalton (1966) reported CMI results on 2245 patients from 14 of the general practices studied by them in their survey. Using a threshold score of 10 on the psychiatric section (M–R section) of the CMI they identified 35·2 per cent of the women and 15·6 per cent of the men as potential cases. However, although the concordance between doctors and the CMI as to which patients constituted a case attained statistical significance, the magnitude of the correlation was only +0·19.

In their discussion of this dismal finding, the authors made three points:

1. The CMI scores of a series of 1484 Maudsley out-patients—all of whom were confirmed as cases at subsequent clinical interview—showed that if the same threshold score of 10 was adopted no fewer than 30 per cent would be classified as probable normals, since their scores fell below this threshold.

2. A test–retest study of the CMI on a group of general practice patients who completed the questionnaire twice, with an interval of 1 year between, showed a high correlation ($r = +0.87$). The authors comment: 'The stability of individual scores over a year is so great as to lead to the suspicion that they may be closely related to personality factors.'

3. They made the point referred to earlier that the CMI score is to some extent dependent upon sociocultural factors, tending to be higher in lower social groups. The general practitioners do not diagnose psychiatric illness

more commonly in lower social groups, and the authors considered it unlikely that psychiatric illness is more prevalent in these groups. They preferred the alternative explanation that cultural factors are involved and that healthy individuals in lower social groups tend to give more 'yes' responses, thus also partially explaining some of the discrepancy observed between the CMI and the general practitioner.

Further objections may be made to the CMI on the grounds that it does not differentiate traits and symptoms, is highly loaded with hypochondriacal items, and is subject to positional response bias and 'yea-saying' bias. The latter points will be dealt with more fully in the next section.

Saslow's New Psychiatric Screening Test

This short, self-administered test deals with possible symptom formation when two emotions—anger and anxiety—are suppressed by the respondent. The test is in two almost identical sections. For each emotion, the respondent is asked whether bottling up his feelings makes him feel ill. If he replies 'yes' or 'sometimes', he is offered a checklist of 18 possible symptoms, and his score on the screening test is obtained by adding the number of symptoms endorsed in each section.

Saslow, Counts, and Dubois (1951) provide validation data for their test by comparing scores on the test with the routine clinical assessments made on a series of 447 patients seen in various hospitals and clinics at St. Louis. Discrimination between those with and without psychiatric disorder was obtained using a threshold score of four or more symptoms to indicate the presence of disorder. Using this threshold the results for the screening test are:

Specificity	95 per cent
Sensitivity	72 per cent
Overall misclassification rate	11 per cent

The overall misclassification rate given here is calculated on the assumption that the prevalence of disorder in the population being examined was 25 per cent. If, to improve the sensitivity of the test, the threshold score is lowered, a sensitivity of 86 per cent could be achieved, but at the expense of an overall misclassification of 26 per cent of the subjects.

When one considers the content of the test it is surprising that it works even this well, since it might have been supposed that it was most suitable for detecting patients with 'psychosomatic' disorders. In fact only 12 per cent of the total group were so diagnosed, and even these had some psychiatric disorder in addition to the 'psychosomatic' illness. It is interesting that a test that does not ask the patient at all about his present symptoms should be so good at detecting disturbances in the current mental state. As the test is worded, a given patient should have the same score irrespective of whether he completes it during a period of sickness or health. One would therefore have expected the test to be giving information about personality traits rather than current illness.

Zung's Self-rating Depression Scale

The scale was compiled by Zung (1965a) and consists of 20 self-descriptive statements to which the respondent is expected to respond on a four-point frequency scale ranging from a 'little of the time' to 'most of the time'. The items were derived from a consideration of three factor analyses of complaints made by depressed patients. When the items are examined it can be seen that the scale is likely to detect other psychiatric illnesses besides depression. It is a little difficult to fit some items—for example 'I still enjoy sex'—on to the frequency scale offered, while many healthy respondents would surely require the response category 'not at all' for items such as, 'I feel that others would be better off if I were dead'. The scale nevertheless resembles the present questionnaire in three respects:

1. Despite its name, it is likely to detect a wide range of patients with minor affective illness.
2. It uses a four-point response scale to overcome the tendency of some respondents to use the middle position of response scales.
3. It consists of some items so phrased that to endorse them indicates health, and others so phrased that to endorse them indicates illness. This introduces a partial correction for the 'overall agreement set' to be discussed in the next section, and a complete correction for the tendency of some respondents to favour a particular position on the scale ('positional bias').

Zung (1965b) confirms the view offered here that other psychiatric patients are likely to have high scores by demonstrating high scores for anxiety states, personality disorders, and 'transient situational adjustment reactions'. No reliability figures are reported, and the 'validity' study is strictly speaking a calibration study. It is disappointing that no items were rewritten or rejected after an item analysis, since some of his items are clearly very much inferior to others as discriminators between the calibration groups.

Finally, one wishes that a validity study had been carried out on a population with some disturbed and some healthy members, with independent assessments by the questionnaire and psychiatric interview. A study by Popoff (1969) comes nearest to this ideal, but all his respondents were judged to be disturbed and the results for the questionnaire are not encouraging. Only 53 per cent of a group of 32 general practice patients who were judged to be depressed at independent psychiatric interview would have been detected by the questionnaire. This survey therefore shows the 'sensitivity' of the questionnaire to be unsatisfactory, but makes no assessment of 'specificity'.

Foulds's Personal Distress Scale

The Personal Distress Scale is a set of items derived from the Symptom-Sign Inventory (SSI) that were found useful in discrimination between healthy respondents and normal people. Foulds (1965) at one time thought that this might be used as a self-administered questionnaire, but the normative data for the Personal Distress Scale are all based on the use of the SSI as an administered interview, as described earlier in the chapter. Philip (1971) is now continuing Foulds's work with the SSI and does not at present intend to develop the Personal Distress Scale as a self-administered questionnaire.

The Middlesex Hospital Questionnaire

This 48-item self-rating scale has been devised by Crown and Crisp (1966) for diagnostic, therapeutic, prognostic, and research purposes. It provides a symptom profile by the use of six 8-item subscales—free floating anxiety, phobias, obsessional, somatic, depressive, and 'hysteric'. The construction of the scale itself seems satisfactory, except that the normal subjects used in the calibration study were all from Social Classes I and II whereas the ill group presumably represented a more usual range, since they were psychiatric outpatients. This may possibly account for the fact that the 'normals' in fact scored higher on 'hysteric' than did the 'ills'.

The MHQ was not designed as a method of case identification, and it seems unlikely that it would be ideal for this purpose. Traits are not distinguished from symptoms, and there is little attempt to measure the severity of the present disturbance. The various subscales are derived on an *ad hoc* basis from clinical categories rather than empirically from psychometric analysis. It is undesirable to use only two criterion groups in the calibration study, and the method of scoring items allows 'overall agreement set' to operate. Finally, if it is to be used for case identification in a community setting it would need to undergo reliability and validity studies, and these have not so far been reported.

Lanyon's Psychological Screening Inventory

This self-administered test consists of 130 statements concerned with personality (e.g. 'high speeds thrill me'; 'I enjoy the theatre') to which the respondent replies 'true' or 'false'. The test is intended as a brief screening device for use in mental health settings, 'where time and psychological skills may be at a premium'. The test generates five subscores which are given somewhat misleading names to 'underplay pathological implications', but which in essence correspond to psychoticism, psychopathic deviance, neuroticism, extroversion, and defensiveness.

The method of construction of the test is described in detail by Lanyon (1970), but although the test is described as a 'screening' test there is no validity study to correlate test scores with independent psychiatric assessments, and it is not possible to compute the sensitivity and specificity of the instrument. In any case, the test does not measure current mental state but seems rather to be a short, multiphasic personality inventory, comparable to the Mini-Mult version of the MMPI (Kincannon, 1968) or to Eysenck's psychoticism–extroversion–neuroticism (PEN) questionnaire. The nearest that the test comes to screening as opposed to personality diagnosis is with the psychoticism scale, where it is said that a high score indicates that the respondent's problems 'warrant formal psychological or psychiatric examination'.

The design of an efficient screening test presents greater psychometric difficulties for psychotic than for neurotic illnesses. One problem is that if the prevalence of a disorder in a population is, for example, 1 per cent, then the effect of declaring everyone 'well' will result in correct decisions 99 per cent of the time. To show that a screening test for this class of illness is effective it is necessary to show that, without declaring an unacceptably large proportion of the population to be potential cases, use of the screening test ultimately results in correct decisions more than 99 per cent of the time. On the evidence at present available, it is impossible to assess the efficiency of this inventory as a screening test either for neurotic or for psychotic illness.

Other Self-administered Questionnaires

There remains a group of self-administered questionnaires mainly designed for assessing change in neurotic patients, and so aimed at assessment of the present mental state rather than at case identification. There is no intrinsic reason why they should not be used for this purpose, but none was specially designed for it and for none have there been validity surveys comparable with those carried out with the present questionnaire.

Hildreth (1946) designed what came to be known as the 'Hildreth Scale' as a 'quantification of the question "how do you feel?"'. It consisted of 175 'typical self-statements' concerned with the mental state and various attitudes, and the validity of the scale was 'considered to be established by the method of construction [of the scale] rather than by a formal validity study'. It is not reassuring to note that a group of 30 surgical patients had higher scores than a group of 40 psychiatric patients.

Parloff, Keliman, and Frank (1954) designed the Johns Hopkins Symptom Distress Checklist in order to assess change in patients undergoing psychotherapy. It is in many ways comparable to the present questionnaire, except that the four-point scale ranges from 'not at all' to 'always' and there is a heavy preponderance of somatic symptoms. Lipman, Covi, Rickels, Uhlenhuth, and Lazar (1968) describe a factor analysis of this checklist and on the basis of this Rickels has produced a 36-item symptom checklist with items selected to represent the five principal factors. Rickels, Goldberg, and Hesbacher (1971) have compared this shortened symptom checklist with the present questionnaire from the viewpoint of screening, and the results will be described in CHAPTER V.

Kellner (1967) and Kellner and Sheffield (1968 *a* and *b*) have described a self-administered form of their 'symptom rating test' that was described in the previous section. The scale was designed to assess 'changes in the symptoms of neurotic adults in therapeutic experiments', and their reliability and validity data relevant to this aim are impressive. In view of the findings to be reported in Chapters III and IV of this monograph, concerning the various ways of scoring the present questionnaire, it is interesting that Kellner (1967) found that 'a distress scale, on which each symptom is rated on more than one dimension, such as frequency, intensity, and duration, does not appear to be more effective . . . than a scale in which each symptom is rated only on one validated dimension' (p. 412).

The SRT was not designed for case identification, and indeed four questions that were shown not to discriminate well between 100 normals and 100 neurotics were left in since the scale 'must be sensitive to *changes* in state, and should be available to the patient for the purpose of self-rating'.

Sheffield (1969) has kindly made available to the author the results of a small study with 43 normal and 40 neurotic persons, and these are given below:

	OVERALL MISCLASSIFICATION RATE %	SENSITIVITY %	SPECIFICITY %
'Checklist' score	13·2	87·5	72
SRT score	14·5	95·0	76·7

When these results are examined it can be seen that they are slightly less good than those found for the present questionnaire [see Chapter IV] yet one would have expected them to be better, since patients with intermediate degrees of disturbance between 'normal' and 'neurotic' were excluded in Sheffield's study.

Conclusion

It has been shown that no scale at present in use is really satisfactory for the purposes of case identification, and that most of them do not distinguish between personality traits and symptoms. Very few take into account the problems of response bias to be considered in the next section, and in general the more rigorously designed validity studies have produced disappointing results for the various scales.

3. *SHORTCOMINGS OF QUESTIONNAIRES*

Reliability of the Informant

It is well known that the patient's account of his symptoms, and even of such relatively objective matters as his observable behaviour, may correspond neither with accounts given by other informants, nor with the clinician's impression at interview. In a thoughtful paper on obsessional personality, Ingram (1961) points out that a person regarded by outside observers as fanatically tidy, may either agree, or rate himself as untidy, or even claim that he doesn't think tidiness more important than others do.

One way of overcoming these difficulties is to collect information from another informant about the patient's behaviour on a separate scale; such a course was suggested by Hogben and Sim (1953) and has actually been carried out in an American study by Katz and Lyerly (1963). This study gives major emphasis to information supplied by another informant, and the item content is strongly slanted towards outwardly observable behaviour and social adjustment. The patient's questionnaire used in this study is by contrast shorter and is given less attention. It consists of the Johns Hopkins Symptom Distress Checklist already discussed in the previous section. In a more recent study in this country, Humphrey (1967) administered a 'functional mood scale' to a series of 40 psychiatric out-patients. Each patient's spouse was later asked to fill in the same scale *with reference to the patient*. He found a correlation of +0·7 between self-assessment and assessment by spouse, and says that this suggests that his scale 'is a reliable as well as a valid measure of neurotic disability'. Unfortunately he is not explicit about the opportunities that each had for knowing what the other had replied to the questions, yet the possibility of collusion is a serious shortcoming of his method.

If we limit ourselves to items which can be answered entirely by the individual respondent, it is worth remembering that we are not concerned about whether the response made by a respondent to a given test is true or false, but only about whether the tendency to answer an item in a given way correlates with severity of disturbance. This is important, since most personality tests depend on the respondents giving 'correct' answers to items, yet as we shall see, research in the past decade has shown that responses to such tests are determined by other variables besides content of the item.

None the less, it seems likely that information given by relatives may ultimately give just as valuable an indication of severity of disturbance as information given by the patient. With this in mind, many of the items in the calibration study are chosen with a view to eventually devising a parallel version of the same questionnaire for an informant.

Defensive Subjects

The response set of 'defensiveness' was described by Walton and Mather (1962) on the basis of their subjects' scores on two questionnaires, one consisting mainly of physical and somatic aspects of health, and the other consisting mainly of psychological items. The former was the Maudsley Medical Questionnaire (MMQ) described by Eysenck (1947) while the latter was the Neuroticism scale from the Maudsley Personality Inventory (MPI) (Eysenck, 1959). Walton and Mather postulated that subjects with a low MPI score but a high MMQ score were 'defensive'; they were able to show that hospitalized neurotic patients with normal MPI scores did indeed tend to have high MMQ scores.

It could be argued from these results that somatic items represent a symptom cluster that does not necessarily correlate with other psychologically orientated symptoms. The finding that there is a group of patients without organic illnesses but with predominantly physical complaints is a clinical commonplace. In the present context the most desirable course of action seems to be to include items with a physical bias as well as those that are entirely psychological. The problem of deciding which items discriminate between various groups of patients can then be left to subsequent statistical analysis.

There is, however, more to the notion of defensiveness than the rather restricted sense in which Walton and Mather use the word. Apart from its use to describe an essentially intrapsychic process, it can also be used to refer to the reluctance of an individual to reveal his inner experiences to other people. Such behaviour may be manifest in a questionnaire situation, or it may be apparent at clinical interview.

Some observers have attempted to measure defensiveness in a questionnaire situation by using the 'K-Scale' of the Minnesota Multiphasic Personality Inventory, and to relate this to physiological variables such as the urinary 17-hydroxycorticosteroid excretion (Tecce, Freedman, and Mason, 1966).

With the questionnaire described in this monograph the nearest equivalent to this kind of 'defensiveness' would be exemplified by those patients who do not admit to any symptoms on the questionnaire, although they are known from other sources of information to suffer from many symptoms. These people could be described as 'false negatives'. It will be possible to study the determinants of this behaviour by describing those patients who are known to be psychiatrically ill but who are found to have low scores.

Abnormal behaviour at interview—suspicious glances, asking whether the interview is *really* confidential, and so on—can be referred to as 'defensiveness' with greater justification. The validity studies of the present questionnaire will provide an opportunity to investigate the interrelationships of this type of behavioural defensiveness and being a 'false negative'.

Overemphatic, Histrionic Subjects

People who spuriously agree to the proposition of illness complement the defensive subjects described above. Polysymptomatic hypochondriacs may score on more items than severely depressed patients, yet we may wish our questionnaire to declare the latter more ill.

This shortcoming can only be reduced; it cannot be eliminated. It is one of the reasons why no questionnaire, however sophisticated, will ever supplant a formal clinical assessment by an expert.

There are various ways of trying to reduce this type of response style. One way is to use a scoring system which gives the same score to a response claiming that a symptom is being experienced in mild degree as to the response that it is experienced in severe degree; while another way is to perform an analysis that will enable us to assign weights to each symptom proportional to its discriminatory power. A final way is to have a number of calibration groups of differing degrees of severity of illness so that the item analysis can reject those items that, although they discriminate well between mildly ill patients and healthy patients, do not discriminate between mildly ill and severely ill patients. All these techniques will be tried in the present study, and we shall adopt those techniques which can be shown to improve discriminatory power of the questionnaire.

Overall Agreement Set

In the last decade clinical psychologists have devoted much attention to overall response sets that may vitiate the results of personality and attitude scales. Undoubtedly one of the most important of these is the so-called 'Overall Agreement Set' (OAS). This refers to the tendency for any given individual to agree or disagree with propositions put to him, irrespective of the content of these propositions. The topic was first studied by Cronbach (1942) who described examination candidates as 'acquiescent' if they tended to guess 'true' when they were in doubt about a proposition that might be either true or false. He suggested that some students could be described as 'acquiescent', just as they might be described as cheerful or friendly.

Couch and Keniston (1960) devised a scale that expressed an individual's tendency to agree as his 'yea-saying score', and described the personality traits that supposedly characterize 'yea-sayers' and 'nay-sayers'. The yea-saying score was shown to have high positive correlations with the number of questions answered 'yes' or 'true' on various well-known personality inventories, so that it is clear that *any* personality or attitude scale, whose responses are so arranged that to reply 'yes' or 'agree' or 'true' to the questions signals possession of the personality attribute concerned, will be heavily contaminated by overall agreement set. One's efforts to measure the personality attribute in question will therefore be impaired in proportion to the extent that agreement set is itself determined by factors that may be irrelevant to that attribute.

An important point to grasp is that content and acquiescence stand in inverse relationship to one another as determinants to a particular test item, so that the more clearly defined the content of a particular item the less important will acquiescence become. Since psychiatric items are all either introspections or descriptions of one's own behaviour one would expect them to be largely determined by content, and only to a lesser extent by overall agreement set.

One way of reducing overall agreement set is to arrange the items so that in half of them agreement signals illness, whereas in the other half agreement signals health. At first sight this would appear to eliminate overall agreement set, but Jackson (1967) has reviewed the highly technical reasons why this is not so. Briefly, items vary in the extent to which each of them is influenced by overall agreement set and by other factors such as content, and social desirability. Merely having equal numbers of 'positive' and 'negative' items does not therefore ensure that overall agreement set will cancel itself out over the whole matrix of test items. Another serious difficulty with 'balanced' scales is that the more a given individual's responses are determined by overall agreement set the greater will be his tendency to be assigned a median position on any particular scale. (If a subject answered 'yes' to every question on a 100-question balanced questionnaire he would be assigned a score of 50.) Now, to the extent that an individual's responses are determined by content, the individual may be said to have a 'true' position on the scale, so that it is clear that with a balanced scale overall agreement set is distorting the 'true' score by skewing it towards the median position of the scale. However, one advantage of making such a 'balanced' questionnaire is that it allows overall agreement set to be assessed independently of content, so that even if the effects of overall agreement set cannot be completely mitigated, at least they can be measured.

Social Desirability

Personality tests have always been exasperatingly disappointing tools for discovering useful information about one's fellow men. Perhaps the main reason for this has been the notion, that has died hard, that the content of an item is the sole determinant of a subject's response to it. It is assumed that people not only *can*, but *will*, reveal data about their private experiences. Discussion has raged for many years round various explanations of the fact that information about a subject revealed by test items may not agree with the subject's observed behaviour. Perhaps the subject is dishonest, is defensive, or habitually agrees with propositions. Thus, various 'lie-scales' and 'fake-good' scales were devised, in addition to those discussed above. In recent years emphasis has changed from 'faking good' to the understandable tendency of people to depict themselves in a good light. Subjects were exhorted to honesty, their anonymity was guaranteed, and various attempts were made to check the consistency of their responses.

In 1953 Edwards dubbed this response set 'social desirability' (SD) and showed that judges' ratings of the social desirability of test items and the probability or their endorsement was no less than $+0.87$. In other words, the more socially desirable any item is, the more likely it is to be answered 'yes'. He does not suggest that 'socially desirable' responses are false, but merely that some people are more likely to respond in this way.

Crowne and Marlow (1964) have pointed out that items on Edwards's SD scale were all drawn originally from clinical scales, and were therefore biased in an abnormal direction in that, for example, an apparent high incidence of social desirability in a population may only reflect a low frequency of neurotic symptoms in that population. They have therefore designed their own social desirability scale, one-half of which consists of items that are culturally acceptable but probably untrue (e.g. 'I have never intensely disliked anyone'), and the other half of items that are probably true but culturally unacceptable (e.g. 'There have been occasions when I took advantage of someone'). Using this scale, Crowne and Marlow have shown that the correlations with the MMPI are much lower than those between the MMPI and the Edwards SD scale (mean correlation 0·29 compared with 0·48). Nevertheless, they are large enough to require some explanation, and the authors suggest that subjects vary in their 'need for approval'; the higher the need, the more likely are individuals to do things to win approval of others: '. . . it is simply not considered desirable in the contemporary social milieu to indicate on a test that one is anxious, frustrated, unhappy and beset by all sorts of strange thoughts and impulses. It is not consistent behaviour if one is dependent upon the acceptance, recognition and approval of others' (Crowne and Marlow, 1964, p. 27).

While this statement may be true for Crowne and Marlow's subjects—who were students in an abnormal psychology class—it is possible that it does not apply to psychiatrically ill patients. An intriguing possibility is that one way in which such people may differ from those who are well, is that they become prepared to make socially undesirable statements about themselves. It seems unlikely that psychiatric patients have different notions about what constitutes a socially desirable response, as Edwards (1957) showed that patients shared similar views on the social desirability of the items on his scale with Skid-row alcoholics, undergraduates, and a group of Norwegians.

Buss (1959) carried out an ingenious investigation into whether the social desirability of the way in which a given item is worded ('item style') determines how often that item is endorsed. The results are complex, but essentially negative. For example, the simple statement, 'I sometimes get into fights' can be rewritten as, 'I can't help getting into fights', or 'Like most people, I get into fights'. The former style will be endorsed less often, and the latter style more often, than the simple statement, yet all three of these styles are shown to have the same social desirability rating. 'I am guilty about getting into fights', on the other hand, is rated as very much more socially desirable, and yet it is endorsed less frequently than 'like most people . . .'. Yet other styles ('I must admit, I . . .'; 'I am tempted to . . .') seem to obey the simple rule, in that they are at once more desirable and more likely to be endorsed.

For our present purposes, we can observe that it is quite impossible to eliminate the response set of social desirability from the questionnaire. It is obvious, for example, that to be preoccupied with suicidal thoughts is at once undesirable and yet correlated with psychiatric ill health.

It is equally clear that some psychiatrically disturbed patients are prepared to reveal socially undesirable information about themselves on a questionnaire. Whether this is because they have less 'need for approval' in Crowne and Marlowe's terms, or because they feel that the expectations of the administrator of the questionnaire are different from those of their neighbours, or because of some other reason, remains a matter for conjecture. What can readily be checked is whether the score of an individual will co-vary on the severity scale here described and on the Crowne and Marlowe SD scale throughout a period of illness.

'End-Users' and 'Middle-Users'

We have seen that it is very difficult to disentangle the responses of subjects to items with bimodal responses from problems of overall agreement set. To respond 'yes', 'true', or 'agree' is characteristic of a 'yea-sayer', as well as a response to the content of an item. Yet if we attempt to escape from this dilemma by using multiple-response scales we enter a new realm of problems.

First, in any rating-scale with an odd number of points it can be shown that respondents will tend to use the middle position—called by Guilford (1936) the 'error of central tendency'.

Even if we confine ourselves to rating-scales with an even number of points, some respondents will show a preference for the more central positions (we will call these the 'middle-users') and others will display a preference for the extreme positions at the ends of the scale (we will call these the 'end-users').

While less is known about the responses of psychiatric patients in this respect than about many other areas of psychophysics, a certain amount of information is gradually becoming available, mainly on the seven-point response scale of the 'Osgood Semantic Differential'. Bopp (1955) showed that schizophrenics tend to use end-positions, and Arthur (1955) confirmed this by showing that deluded patients tended to use end-points while normal subjects tended to use middle-points; in contrast, phobics might adopt either response style.

Neuringer (1963) showed that neuropsychiatric patients tended to use extreme positions more than normals, and Marks (1965) confirmed these findings; he showed that both obsessionals and psychopaths used mid-positions less, and end-positions more, than normals.

We may conclude that it seems likely that psychiatric patients will tend to use end-positions more than normal people, but we do not know whether the use of end-positions is made more likely as illness becomes more severe. This is one of the reasons why a scoring method has been devised that eliminates this response bias, although admittedly it does this only by losing information.

Positional Bias

Anyone filling in a questionnaire may tend to favour responses in a particular position on the printed page. This motor-response set has been known for many years, and is easily avoided by presenting the various response sequences in random order. However, many questionnaires do not take account of this error, so that in the CMI for example, the yea-saying hypochondriacs whom we would expect to score highly, find that they can signal agreement to an item with a response that is always on the same side.

Scoring problems

If a questionnaire uses multiple responses to each item, then it is usual for the degree of response to be scored.

Let us consider an example:

ITEM A

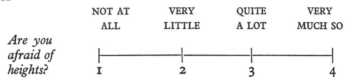

Two problems immediately arise about such an item. From the respondent's point of view, the 'conceptual distance' between positions 1 and 2 (i.e. between having and not having a neurotic symptom) may be much greater than between positions 3 and 4 (i.e. between varying degrees of intensity of the symptom). Yet they are presented to him on a linear scale, as though the distance between each was the same. From the investigator's point of view, the dilemma is similar yet even more acute. If a linear scoring method is used—for example, the positions 1, 2, 3, and 4 each receive a score of that number—it may well be that scores are now being assigned which do not produce optimum discrimination between groups of respondents.

Let us now compare responses to this item with responses to another item, for example:

ITEM B

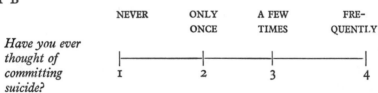

It is equally clear that the distance between 1 and 2 should be greater than that between 3 and 4; but a fresh problem now arises when the score on Item A is added to the score on Item B. With the linear scoring method being considered we are assuming that not only are the intervals between response positions on any particular item all equal, but that they are also equal to the intervals between response positions on *other* items. In other words, the distance between A3 and A4 is assumed to be equal to the distance between B1 and B2.

We shall refer to the first sort of scoring problem as one occurring *between columns*, and the second sort as one occurring *between rows*. Even if we construct a non-linear scale varying between 0 and unity for each item, and thus solve our problem between columns, we are left with the problem between rows.

Theoretically, the problem could, of course, be solved by separately computing a weighted score for each response position on each item separately.

Yet this would involve immense computational labour, and would leave us with a questionnaire that was very difficult to score.

These multiple-response scales are usually referred to as 'Likert Scales' after Rensis Likert, the American psychometrician who introduced them. Despite the problems associated with their use, they also have some advantages which cannot be set aside at this stage of the investigation. For this reason it has been decided to administer the questionnaire in a form that permits scoring by multiple-response scale methods as well as by the method to be described in the next chapter.

Graphic Rating-scales

These have been described in detail by Guilford (1936) and are similar to the multiple-response scales discussed above except that the subject makes his response by making a mark on a continuous line drawn above the possible responses. Although obviously allowing a greater freedom in response, the problems of positioning the various responses—like beads on a string—and weighting the final response, are as great as before.

One partial solution to this problem is merely to define the ends of the scale, as in the following example:

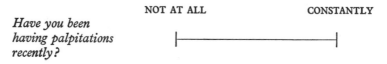

Have you been having palpitations recently?   NOT AT ALL   CONSTANTLY

This method is sometimes called a 'thermometer scale'. However, the idea of a thermometer, and the concept of points along it, require a degree of sophistication only attained by a proportion of the population. Many items either cannot be fitted on to the idea of a thermometer at all, or can only be fitted with great difficulty. Items have to be designed with great care, as the response dimensions of intensity and duration are easily confused. The problems of end- and middle-users remain unsolved with this scoring method.

Because of the difficulties associated with each of the methods discussed above, and bearing in mind the recent work on response sets described earlier in this chapter, a new item layout and scoring method has been specially designed for this questionnaire. This will be described in the following chapter.

CHAPTER III

THE DEVELOPMENT OF THE QUESTIONNAIRE

1. *INTRODUCTION*

WE may now re-examine the aims of the study in the light of the findings described in the previous chapter. There is evidently a need for a new questionnaire which can serve as a screening instrument in community surveys and identify 'potential cases', leaving the task of identifying 'actual cases' to psychiatric interview.

Since we are concerned with severity of disturbance in the present and not with the lifelong possession or otherwise of neurotic traits, the items consist of symptoms like abnormal feelings and thoughts, and aspects of observable behaviour. Respondents are therefore asked to compare the extent to which they experience each item in the present with the extent to which they *usually* experience it.

The test items therefore stress the 'here and now' situation, and pay no attention to how the individual has felt or behaved in the past. The emphasis is not on what the individual is 'usually like', but always on how his present state differs from his usual state. This not only has the effect of giving prominence to symptoms at the expense of personality traits, but also incidentally makes the questionnaire less subject to 'overall agreement set' since the respondent does not have to respond 'yes', 'agree', or 'true'. Moreover, as far as possible the items are so worded that even if they *were* answered with the response 'yes', half would signal illness and half would signal health. In practice it is very much easier to think of propositions where agreement signals illness than those where agreement signals health, but a 'balanced' questionnaire with equal numbers of each type of item, is one of a number of possibilities that will be examined at a later stage.

Since psychiatric illness is not a unitary concept, it may well be that to attempt to express the degree of disturbance by a single number is to attempt the impossible, even if the psychoses are excluded. Perhaps, like the somatotype, degree of disturbance should be expressed as a profile of numbers rather than as a single number. Since there are no very strong *a priori* reasons for preferring one course to another, this problem will be tackled by means of a principal components analysis.

The questionnaire is not a mere complaints inventory for two reasons. First, it consists only of items that can be shown to discriminate well between groups of respondents with different degrees of severity of illness. Secondly, an item is only counted as being present if the patient considers that its presence represents a departure from his 'usual self'.

Finally, the questionnaire aims to provide normative data about the symptoms and signs that define non-psychotic psychiatric illness in an English population. While, for example, the item, 'Do you often feel miserable and blue?' may well provide discrimination between groups of American patients, we need to know the best way to ask about common psychiatric symptoms in order to obtain optimum discrimination in an English setting.

There are a number of reasons why no attempt has been made to obtain information from an informant in the present study. In the first place, an informant is not always obtainable, so limiting the test to the respondent will ensure a greater number of cases. Secondly, in community work many people may resent their nearest relative being asked to answer intimate questions about their personal lives, and so a fair number of refusals might be anticipated. Thirdly, in the interests of simplicity it seems advisable to produce a respondent's questionnaire before embarking on the design of a possible supplementary questionnaire. Finally, the stipulated aim of the study was to obtain a measure which would be short and easy to administer as well as being acceptable, and so it is clearly desirable to keep it as simple as possible.

2. METHOD—(i) THE CONSTRUCTION OF A LONG FORM OF THE QUESTIONNAIRE

Layout and Method of Scoring Each Item

Each item consists of a question asking whether the respondent has recently experienced a particular symptom or item of behaviour on a scale ranging from 'less than usual' to 'much more than usual'. By avoiding a bimodal response scale the errors due to overall agreement set can be reduced, and by having an even number of response categories the 'error of central tendency' described in the previous chapter is eliminated. An example of an item showing two possible scoring methods is shown below:

Have you recently been feeling sad and gloomy?	COLUMN 1 Less so than usual	COLUMN 2 No more than usual	COLUMN 3 Rather more than usual	COLUMN 4 Much more than usual
LIKERT SCORE:	0	1	2	3
GHQ SCORE:	0	0	1	1

This four-point response scale may be scored in two ways. It can be treated as a multiple-response scale or 'Likert scale' and have weights assigned to each position, which are shown in the above example as the 'Likert Score'.

Alternatively, it can be treated as a bimodal response scale so that only pathological deviations from normal signal possession of the item. This method of scoring has been called 'GHQ Score', after the name of the questionnaire—the General Health Questionnaire—and is also shown in the above example. It is not only a very simple method of scoring, but has the advantage that it eliminates any errors due to 'end-users' and 'middle-users', since they will score the same irrespective of whether they tend to prefer Columns 1 and 4 or Columns 2 and 3 to indicate possession or non-possession of the item in question. This advantage is gained only at the cost of losing information, and in order to see if it is justified by results the two scoring methods will be compared at a later stage.

What the GHQ scoring method does in effect is to reduce the error caused by the response sets associated with bimodal response scales by making each item masquerade as a Likert scale. But as the response scale is *not* in fact a Likert scale, we entirely eliminate the errors associated with these scales, which were discussed in the previous chapter.

This scoring method is original to this work, and is so fundamental to what follows that it is perhaps worth listing the advantages and disadvantages associated with its use.

Advantages of the GHQ Scoring Method

1. *Reduction of bias associated with bimodal response scales.* What has come to be known as overall agreement set, including 'yes-saying', 'truth-saying' and 'agree-saying' bias, is minimized by the form of the response scale. This bias can be further reduced by wording the items so that, even if a respondent were to answer them mentally with 'yea' or 'nay', some would signal illness and some health.

2. *Elimination of bias associated with Likert Scales.* (i) The most obvious advantage is that the 'between-columns' scoring problem, as described in the previous chapter, disappears entirely. (ii) The problems associated with the response habits of middle-users and end-users are also eliminated, as described above. (iii) It will be possible to compute weights for each item by using a discriminant function analysis, and thus solve what was described as the 'between-row' scoring problem in the previous chapter. When this has been done it will be possible to compare the results of scoring the questionnaire using separate weights with the results of using the GHQ and Likert scoring methods already described.

3. *Elimination of the 'error of central tendency'.* This has been achieved by the use of a four-point scale which forces response to the left or right.

4. *Elimination of errors associated with 'positional bias'.* It will ultimately be possible to eliminate this source of error by random allocation of the 'ill side' of the response scale to the left and right. This will not be done until the questionnaire has been shortened by the procedures described in CHAPTER IV —while it remains at its present length (140 items), the 'ill responses' have all been printed on the right side of the response scale, as this has been found to diminish fatigue in the respondent.

Disadvantage of the GHQ Scoring Method

The GHQ scoring procedure undoubtedly entails a loss of potential information, and some of this lost information may be valuable. For this reason the questionnaire will be scored by Likert scoring methods and weighted scores in addition to the GHQ method, so that the respective advantages and disadvantages of each method can be compared to greater effect.

The Source of the Items

Investigators who have used factor analysis to help solve psychometric problems have been criticized in the past for their relative lack of interest in the tests used, in contrast to their preoccupation with the statistical manipulations used to derive, and later to speculate about, the factors (Heim, 1954).

The importance of having some rationale for selecting the original items in any test battery has been stressed by distinguished psychometricians. Thus, Remmers (1954) writes: 'The value of the results of the factor analytic method of determining traits also depends on the validity of the measures of psychological behaviour which compose the original battery of tests analysed.' Guttman (1945) argues along similar lines when he states that item selection and factor analysis of a sample of items on a sample of persons is not by itself adequate unless there is 'a cogent initial argument based on content' (of the items).

Fortunately, preliminary work has already been done on possible areas likely to be helpful. Gurin, Veroff, and Feld (1960) and Veroff, Feld, and Gurin (1962) studied a sample of 2460 Americans who were thought to be representative of the non-hospitalized population. A smaller sample of 542 women and 255 men were each extensively interviewed in each of 19 areas which comprehensively covered all possible aspects of adjustment and 'felt distress'. A factor analysis on this imposing mass of material yielded four factors for both sexes:

1. 'Felt psychological disturbance.'
2. 'Unhappiness.'
3. 'Social inadequacy.'
4. 'Lack of identity.'

For the men only there was a fifth factor, 'physiological distress'. It was possible to extract from these workers' book items which were suitable for inclusion in the present questionnaire and which had high saturation on these factors, especially the first three mentioned.

Abrahamson and his associates' (1965) 'Ten Key Questions' from the Cornell Medical Index, already described in CHAPTER II, were also rewritten especially for the questionnaire.

Consequent upon the distinction between symptoms and signs of illness and personality traits, items were selected which would stress the changing aspects of disease. Furthermore, items measuring aspects of behaviour which are observable by others were included. The idea behind this was to include items which might later be used in an 'informant's questionnaire'.

On the basis of the work discussed above, and on the clinical experience of several psychiatrists with whom the project was discussed, four main areas were chosen in which the search for items was to be conducted.

The first area was depression, and this included items covering 'unhappiness' in Veroff and his co-workers' sense, as well as items adapted from the 'N' scale of the CMI (which is the subscale that measures depression).

The second area was anxiety and 'felt psychological disturbance'. Some items concerned with anxiety and 'paranoid irritability' were suggested by items in the CMI while the notion of 'felt psychological disturbance' not only included items suggested by Veroff and his co-workers' study, but was extended to embrace the notion of a lack of 'role-satisfaction'. The notion of 'role-satisfaction' is discussed by Fried and Lindemann (1961), who attribute the idea to Talcott Parsons (1959), and the items concerned with it were specially written for the present study.

The third area was objectively observable behaviour, and consisted of items that could be reported on either by the respondent or by another informant. Items bearing on social impairment and Veroff and his associates' 'social inadequacy' were included here.

The fourth area was 'hypochondriasis', and consisted of a wide variety of superficially 'organic' items, many of which were adapted from the CMI which is very heavily loaded with such items.

Having decided upon the areas, an extensive search was made for as many items as possible. In addition to the scales and investigations already mentioned, ideas for items were obtained from Taylor's Manifest Anxiety Scale, Eysenck's Maudsley Personality Inventory, and the Minnesota Multiphasic Personality Inventory. All the items were rewritten in the form already discussed. About 30 items not suggested by any of the scales and inventories that were examined were specially written for the present study.

Final Selection and Arrangement of the Items

In selecting items for the questionnaire the field was not only narrowed by the exclusion of personality traits, but was also severely limited by the fact that all items had to be applicable to the entire population. While this was essential, it was also perhaps the most unfortunate restriction on the study. Many areas, obviously relevant, had to be dropped because of these considerations. Although one's relations with one's spouse, parents, children, employer, and with one's colleagues may all be sensitive indicators of mental disturbance, none of them can be included as items since none has general applicability. Eventually it was decided to adopt non-committal expressions such as 'those close to you' for a number of items that seemed too valuable to drop at such an early stage of the investigation, even though it was clearly a possibility that some individuals might consider themselves so isolated that there was no one close to them.

Where necessary, items from other tests that were double-barrelled were split into separate items, and some items were regretfully discarded because they did not permit a homogeneous response, using the four-point response scale already described (less than usual / same as usual / rather more than usual / much more than usual).

When these procedures had been carried out there were 140 items left, about equally divided between the four areas. These were then separately written out on 140 cards, and various subjects were invited to sort them into piles of those that 'seemed similar'. It was found that there was a broad measure of agreement about this, and the cards were eventually arranged in seven groups of approximately 20 each.

There were two related reasons for this procedure. The first was to diminish fatigue—as it was thought that answering 140 personal questions might be an imposing task for anyone who was both emotionally disturbed and poorly educated, as some of the respondents were bound to be. The second reason was that it seemed unwarranted to impose preconceived notions upon our respondents about which items were related to one another, by presenting them in the four original 'areas'.

It was not always easy to give a collective name to the groups derived by the card-sorting procedure, but they could be thought of under the following rough headings:

A. General health and central nervous system (17 items)
B. Cardiovascular, neuromuscular, and gastrointestinal (18 items)
C. Sleep and wakefulness (19 items)
D. Observable behaviour—personal behaviour (22 items)
E. Observable behaviour—relations with others (20 items)
F. Subjective feelings—inadequacy, tension, temper, etc. (25 items)
G. Subjective feelings—mainly depression and anxiety (19 items)

It must be emphasized that these are in no way subscales of the test, and the items could have been sorted out in many different ways. Many of the items could be fitted equally well into several categories, but were sorted so that the groups were of approximately equal size.

The complete questionnaire will be found in APPENDIX I, and it will be seen that the subheadings given above are not printed on the questionnaire; the various sets of questions merely being assigned letters of the alphabet from A to G. The questionnaire starts with questions with a somatic bias, as it is presented to respondents as a General Health Questionnaire. As one proceeds through the questionnaire the items become more overtly psychiatric, and questions that are potentially the most disturbing, such as those about suicidal ideas, are left to the end. The reason for this was that respondents might be so upset by questions of this sort that they would abandon the questionnaire, and it would obviously be better if this occurred at the very end. It turned out to be a groundless fear, however, as no respondents failed to answer these questions, or stopped the questionnaire at that point.

Finally, at the end of the questionnaire the patient is thanked for his co-operation, and asked to answer two more questions:

I. He is asked how fatiguing he found the questionnaire, with a four-point response scale:

	1	2	3	4
How tiring did you find this questionnaire?	No bother at all	I got rather tired towards the end but think my answers were accurate	Tired towards the end and may not have been accurate	Very tiring. Many of the items difficult

2. He is asked to rate himself on a five-point scale of illness, which was so designed as to allow comparison with the rating made about each patient by the doctor:

	1	2	3	4	5
Do you think that you are at all ill?	Healthier and more stable than average	About average	Slightly more nervous or ill than average	Fairly ill: would be helped by medical treatment	Very ill: need to be in hospital

A Pilot Experiment

As soon as the questionnaires became available, 35 subjects well known to the author were each asked to complete one. Seven were non-patients and 28 were patients under the author's care at the Maudsley Day Hospital and St. Francis' Observation Unit. When the subjects' scores were plotted against prior assessments of the severity of psychiatric illness it was shown that the questionnaire produced excellent discrimination between the five severity groups used, irrespective of the scoring method adopted.

No group of patients found the test unduly fatiguing and the severely ill group did not find the test more fatiguing than the non-patients taken as a group. A final use of the pilot study was that it allowed many typing errors and items whose wording was unclear to be put right.

METHOD—(ii) THE CALIBRATION OF THE LONG FORM OF THE QUESTIONNAIRE

General Considerations Concerning Calibration

At first sight it might seem adequate to perform the item analysis of the questionnaire using two demographically matched calibration groups—those who were well, and those who were psychiatrically ill. However, there are fundamental objections to this procedure.

If the psychiatrically ill group consisted only of severely disturbed patients, then it is likely that items would be lost that would have discriminated between people who were well and those who were only mildly ill. Yet these are the very items that must find a place in the questionnaire if it is to be of use in the detection of potential cases in the community. Conversely, if only mild cases were used in the calibration study, then the questionnaire would not be a sensitive measure of various degrees of psychiatric disturbance.

It is possible, and even likely, that the querulous polysymptomatic patient mentioned in CHAPTER II has different complaints from a patient with, for example, a severe depression, whom we may want to consider as the more severely ill. Since the former patient would be in the 'mild' calibration group, and the latter patient in the 'severe' calibration group, there is a chance that a three-point calibration procedure would provide weights that would assist in discriminating between these patients. It follows from these arguments that at least three calibration groups should be used.

Indeed, it is easy to see that, theoretically, the more calibration groups there are the better, since the more points there are the fewer are the curves that can be fitted on to them. If there were some valid way of discriminating between a larger number of calibration groups it would be possible to choose only those items that had an even, steep gradient of response from health to severe illness. However, in practice there are great difficulties involved in defining calibration groups in such a way that there is no question of overlap between the groups.

Since there is no reliable criterion against which severity can be judged, conditions must be defined for inclusion in each calibration group in such a way that any individual patient would be assigned to the same group irrespective of the varying standards of the clinician who was rating him. When four groups were tried (normals, mildly ill, moderately ill, and severely ill) it was found that there was often disagreement about which group an individual should be assigned to.

Eventually, three calibration groups were adopted, since it was found that with this arrangement there was no overlap between the groups. It must be made clear that these groups have been defined in such a way that a large number of individuals are likely to fall between the groups—but this seems justifiable in a calibration study.

The three calibration groups chosen were 'normals', 'mildly ill', and 'severely ill' psychiatric patients.

If the final questionnaire is to consist of perhaps 50 or 60 items, then at least 80 of the 'best' items are needed for the principal components analysis. Since there must be more people than items in each calibration group, this means having at least 100 subjects in each group.

The Severely Ill Group

To be included in this group patients had to satisfy two criteria; they had to be patients on the disturbed admission ward of a mental hospital and the doctor looking after them had to rate them '5' on the following five-point scale:

1	2	3	4	5
Completely well	Such complaints as he/she has do not merit psychiatric help	Mildly ill— needs some psychiatric help. Quite all right as an out-patient	Moderately ill. In-patient care probably helpful although not essential	Severely ill. In-patient psychiatric care essential on grounds of mental state

In practice the patients were given the questionnaire by the Sister or Charge Nurse on the wards on the basis of instructions pinned up in each ward, which stated that patients had to be 'severely disturbed' to be suitable for the questionnaire. The notice stated that patients who were schizophrenic, hypo-manic, or demented were unsuitable for the study, and went on to enumerate the diagnostic labels that were suitable. The number of patients who were considered suitable by the Charge Nurse, but were rated as '4' or less by the psychiatrist, varied from unit to unit. It was difficult to say whether this number reflected the ideas of the psychiatrist concerned as to which patients should best be treated as in-patients, or the ideas of the nurse as to what constituted 'severe disturbance'. Although they are therefore to some extent a heterogeneous group, it is unlikely that many of them could be rated in the middle calibration group even if they discharged themselves from hospital and were rated by a different psychiatrist on the same scale.

As larger numbers of questionnaires were collected, the twin hazards of defensiveness and exaggeration already discussed were seen. Three patients were questioned because, as they became well known to the author in the Observation Ward, there was no reason to doubt the initial rating of 'severe disturbance', yet their total scores were well below the mean of the group.

The first patient was a man who turned out to have a psychotic depression. On closer examination, he was an exceedingly shy, secretive man, and was deeply ashamed of mental illness and the fact that he was now in hospital.

The second was a man with a hysterical personality who turned out to be an evasive liar about all personal topics: the questionnaire responses were here merely part of a wider pattern.

The third was a social worker whose husband had left her and had just attempted suicide after a drinking bout. She stated that the questionnaire was probably 'an important part of my treatment—it may mean my going on to another hospital'. This lady was acquainted with the area mental hospital, and strongly motivated to make the staff suppose that she had now recovered so that she would not be sent there.

It is less easy to show that some patients exaggerate, but two points suggested that it might occur. Many young people with personality disorders handed in questionnaires with high scores, but the doctors looking after them did not rate them as requiring in-patient care. While this could equally be due to error in the doctor's rating, it seems unlikely that all the cases of high scoring were due to this. The other point is that alcoholics in the Observation Ward scored very highly as a group—often higher than patients with formal psychiatric illness of some severity. While one cannot conclude from this that alcoholics tend to overstate their case, it is a possibility worth bearing in mind.

The patients were collected over a period of 6 months at the Observation Ward of St. Francis' Hospital, at the Villa Ward of the Maudsley Hospital, from Cane Hill Hospital, and from St. John's Hospital, Stone, with the kind permission of the consultants in charge of the various units.

The Mildly Ill Group

To be included in this group a patient had to be both attending the Out-patient Department of the Maudsley Hospital and rate '3' on the doctor's rating-scale. It will be recalled that this rating reads 'Mildly ill—needs some psychiatric help. Quite all right as an out-patient.' In practice this rating occasionally caused some difficulty because of its double-barrelled nature, since there is also a group of patients who were considered 'moderately ill' and yet 'quite all right as an out-patient'. Where this confusion occurred the patients were usually discussed with the rater by the author. The test question in these cases was, 'Would you admit this patient if you had a hospital bed available?' If the answer to this question was 'yes' the patient was rated as '4' and lost to the study, while if the answer was 'no' he was usually rated as '3' and included. The case notes of each patient attending out-patients in December 1966 were examined, and as far as possible the questionnaire was administered to consecutive attenders of the department who were diagnosed as other than schizophrenia, hypomania, or dementia.

Four forms were pinned into each of the case notes selected. The doctor's rating-scale—already shown in the section describing the severe group—and a short letter explaining the questionnaire to the doctor were pinned to the front cover, and the questionnaire itself was clipped to a short letter explaining the nature of the survey to the patient. The last two were handed to each patient on his arrival at the Out-patient Department by the Registry staff, and the questionnaires were completed in out-patients as the patients waited to see their doctors. The opening instructions were only very slightly different from those used in the severe group, since the patients were promised anonymity.

As soon as each questionnaire was returned and matched with the doctor's rating the demographic data and diagnosis were copied on to a separate sheet, and the front page of the questionnaire containing the demographic data was torn off. Thereafter the questionnaire was identifiable only by a number, and so the promise of anonymity was kept.

As might be expected, most of the patients attending for routine out-patient appointments at a general psychiatric clinic were rated as '3', so that by the time 100 cases rated as '3' had been collected there were only six rated as '2' and five cases rated as '4'. No cases were rated as '1', and the two cases rated '5' were both admitted at once.

Bearing in mind the finding that 30 per cent of first attenders at the Maudsley Out-patient Department scored 10 or less on the M–R scale of the CMI (Shepherd, Cooper, Brown, and Kalton, 1966) it is interesting to compare the incidence of low scores in the present study. Of the 100 subjects selected for the study 10 per cent scored less than 5, and 15 per cent scored 10 or less. (The score referred to is the GHQ Score, or total number of items endorsed in either Column 3 or Column 4.) This finding is especially interesting in view of the fact that patients attending follow-up clinics are generally

TABLE 4

CLINICAL DIAGNOSES ASSIGNED TO THE 'MILDLY ILL' AND 'SEVERELY ILL' GROUPS OF PATIENTS

DIAGNOSIS	MILD GROUP	SEVERE GROUP
Depression (all types)	61	60
Anxiety state	10	6
Phobias, agoraphobia	11	0
Hysteria	3	4
Obsessional neurosis	6	1
Personality disorder (unspecified)	20	33
Schizoid personality	0	3
Alcoholism (including DTs)	3	12
Drug addiction	1	7
Psychopath	2	2
Miscellaneous	18	11
Totals	*135*	*139*

thought of as being *less* disturbed than those attending out-patients for the first time.

Several of the patients in this small group of low scorers were being seen because of illness that they had had in the past rather than for a disturbance that was manifest at present: the low score here represented an accurate assessment of their mental states. Another group of low scorers were patients who had had phobic symptoms for some years, and although they still had some symptoms they were well used to them, and the symptoms usually caused little trouble. The psychiatrist who saw them often commented that they were in a good phase of their illness. These patients responded 'no worse than usual' to items covering their symptoms, and therefore scored zero.

The diagnoses assigned to each patient in the two 'ill' calibration groups are given in TABLE 4. The totals add up to more than 100 since many patients received more than one diagnosis. The various types of depression have been lumped together since many patients are merely given a diagnosis of 'depression' or 'affective illness' without a more exact diagnosis being attempted.

(It was possible to check on the types of depression found among the severe group at a later stage by checking on the ICD diagnosis coded on their discharge: 73 per cent had reactive depression, 27 per cent psychotic depression. Of the 61 depressed out-patients only 38 could be classified, but of these 90 per cent had reactive depression. It is perhaps worth noting in this context that despite its name, the questionnaire effectively detects both types of depression. Patients with an acute schizophrenic episode usually also have high scores, but patients with chronic schizophrenia, hypomania, and organic states are usually missed.)

It can be seen from TABLE 4 that the diagnostic structure of the two groups is broadly similar. The differences are relatively slight, and are accounted for by the nature of the groups—it is easy to understand that phobics and obsessionals are more commonly found in out-patients than in the disturbed wards, and that the converse is true for patients with drug addiction and delirium tremens.

The 'Normals'

Although it would obviously have been desirable to define this group on the same dual principles as the previous group, it was not considered practical in terms of available time to arrange for a psychiatrist to interview normal people, and having decided which should be rated 'completely well' on the five-point scale to persuade a demographically matched group of 100 of them to complete the questionnaire.

No entirely satisfactory criteria exist for deciding what should constitute a normal person, and the solution adopted for the present study seemed the most satisfactory of the many alternatives considered.

Five professional interviewers were employed to carry out a door-to-door survey in the community to obtain 'normal' respondents. These interviewers were full-time employees of a commercial firm, National Opinion Polls Limited, they were all young people between the ages of 25 and 35, and most of them were graduates. The author was able to brief them at length, and National Opinion Polls checked on a 10 per cent sample of the respondents approached by the interviewers.

The task of the interviewers was to administer a structured interview to each individual they approached, and if they were suitable on various criteria set out below, to persuade them to fill in a copy of the questionnaire. In the interviewer's briefing session the project was explained to the interviewer, and the screening interview was gone over with them in detail. Each interviewer was given a sheet of 'instructions', which reminded them of the important points made in the briefing session.

The structured interview itself is set out in APPENDIX 2. The aim of this interview was to establish on six criteria whether the individual could be accepted as a respondent. It was considered important to do this without using criteria which were themselves similar to items in the questionnaire.

The six criteria were as follows:

1. Each individual was asked to rate his 'general health' as good, fair, or poor. Those rating it as 'poor' were rejected.
2. Individuals who had been to their own doctor for more than one spell of sickness in the past 3 months were rejected.
3. Those who were on 'nerve tablets', or who were on *regular* tablet treatment prescribed by their doctor, were rejected.

TABLE 5

REPLIES OF THE 100 RESPONDENTS COMPRISING THE 'NORMAL GROUP' TO THE SIX QUESTIONS IN THE INTERVIEW, COMPARED WITH THOSE OF THE 25 PATIENTS REJECTED BY THE INTERVIEW

		ACCEPTED	REJECTED
1. General health rated as:	GOOD	95	
	FAIR	5	
	POOR		9
		100	
2. How often they have attended doctor in previous 12 weeks:	NOT AT ALL	79	
	ONCE	21	
	MORE THAN ONCE		2
		100	
3. Taking medicines or tablets:	NONE	91	
	SELF-MEDICATORS	3	
	TRIVIAL	6	
	REGULAR, or 'PSYCHIATRIC'		5
		100	
4. Time off work:	NOT APPLICABLE	21	
	NONE	76	
	LESS THAN 2 WEEKS	3	
	MORE THAN 2 WEEKS		1
		100	
5. Anything your health stops you from doing?	NOTHING	95	
	TRIVIAL REPLIES	5	
	SERIOUS LIMITATIONS		0
		100	
6. Nerve trouble, persistent insomnia or anything like that?	NO	95	
	TRIVIAL REPLIES	5	
	YES		8
		100	
		TOTAL ACCEPTED = 100	TOTAL REJECTED = 25

4. Those who had lost more than 2 weeks' work in the past 3 months were rejected.
5. The answer to the question 'Does your health stop you from doing anything?' was recorded.
6. Those who admitted 'any kind of nerve trouble', or said they suffered from persistent insomnia, were rejected. Moreover, after the interviewer had asked them if they suffered from nerve trouble or persistent insomnia, he then asked 'or anything like that?' and recorded their reply to this 'open-ended' question.
7. A seventh criterion was derived from the last page of the questionnaire, when the respondent was invited to rate himself on a scale of illness. Those respondents who rated themselves 'slightly more nervous or ill than average' were also excluded from the calibration group.

It must be emphasized that this self-rating is in no sense a test item, and can be thought of as a pencil and paper version of Question 6 in the structured interview.

In order to obtain a group of 100 respondents matched to the other groups for age, sex, and social class, the interviewers approached 162 subjects by door-to-door survey in the London area in January 1967. The results of this survey can best be given as a series of tables [see TABLES 5 and 6].

It should be noted that no one is recorded as having been rejected for more than one reason, because the screening interview was stopped as soon as there were grounds for rejecting the respondent.

If the overall results of this survey are considered, it is interesting to see how many people, approached more or less at random, satisfy what might be thought to be the fairly stringent requirements of this study.

TABLE 6

CLASSIFICATION OF THE 162 INDIVIDUALS INTERVIEWED BY THE INTERVIEWERS IN THE COMMUNITY

	NUMBER	PERCENTAGE
Accepted for the study	100	61·7
Accepted by the interview, but rejected for matching purposes	5	3·1
Accepted, but rejected because questionnaires were incomplete	3	1·9
Accepted by interview, but refused to fill up questionnaire	19	11·7
Rejected by interview	25	15·4
Rejected by self-rating on questionnaire	10	6·2
Totals	*162*	*100*

It can be seen from this table that the structured interview itself accepted 84·6 per cent of the individuals approached. Of the 137 individuals accepted by the interviewers, completed questionnaires could be obtained in 115 (84 per cent). Of these respondents handing back completed questionnaires only 8·7 per cent would have to be rejected because of an unsatisfactory self-rating.

The demographic data on the three calibration groups are shown as APPENDIX 3.

3. RESULTS

The Item Analysis

The first stage in the treatment of the results consisted of gathering together the responses made by the three groups to each item separately. This laborious procedure necessitated regrouping 42,600 items of information, so that for any given item it was possible to compare the responses made by the groups of the four-point scale. The entire item analysis will be found as APPENDIX 4.

If these results are examined it is at once clear that the majority of items discriminate well between the groups. An ideal item should be responded to by as few as possible of the 'normals', and by as many as possible of the 'severely ill', with the 'mildly ill' at some intermediate position. Thus the gradient of response should be both linear and steep.

TABLE 7

EXAMPLE OF AN IDEAL ITEM WITH A STEEP, LINEAR GRADIENT

ITEM F19	GROUP	REFUSED	1	2	3	4	GHQ SCORE
Have you recently	NORMAL	0	8	90	2	0	2
felt unable to	MILD	1	6	55	25	13	38
face your	SEVERE	0	5	22	33	40	73
problems?							

It will be recalled that the GHQ Score refers to any response in Columns 3 or 4: in the present context it is therefore obtained by merely adding the numbers in Columns 3 and 4 together. If we consider the GHQ Score, the gradient can be expressed by the figures 2–38–73. There are a large number of such items with steep linear gradients, especially towards the end of the questionnaire where the content of the items is overtly psychiatric.

On the other hand, a number of the items can be seen to be poor items merely on visual inspection of the data. Only three items did not have a gradient at all—the item about worrying over gaining weight (8–19–10), the item about shortness of breath (4–35–30), and that about blushing (2–8–7). These were all rejected. Two further items were rejected which did have a gradient between 'normals' and 'mildly ill', but had no gradient between 'mildly ill' and 'severely ill'; these were: 'being afraid to go out alone' (0–21–21), and 'losing one's temper' (7–42–42). This left 135 items, all of which had a progressive gradient of response.

The next stage was the elimination of items which, though they had an even gradient, had a slope that was too low, as shown in TABLE 8.

TABLE 8

EXAMPLE OF AN ITEM REJECTED BECAUSE OF A 'LOW SLOPE'

ITEM B15	GROUP	REFUSED	1	2	3	4	GHQ SCORE
Have you recently	NORMAL	0	83	11	6	0	6
had griping pains	MILD	1	69	18	8	4	12
in your belly?	SEVERE	2	56	18	15	9	24

The gradient of this item can be obtained by subtracting the first figure from the last: so that in this example with the numbers 6–12–24 the gradient would be 18. (This simple method of calculating the gradient makes the assumption that the three numbers lie on a straight line. Although this is not always true, the method gives a sufficiently good approximation for the present purpose.)

It was decided to exclude all those items with a gradient of less than 40. When this was done 34 more items were excluded. Two more could have been excluded but were not, since their gradient was more than 30 and none of the normal population endorsed them. They were retained because items that are responded to by none of the normal population are from a statistical point of view of special value as case identifiers. The two items were 'hands shaking and trembling' (0–15–39) and 'afraid that you might collapse in a public place' (0–21–31).

Just as items that none of the normal population responds to are valuable, so items that many of the normal population possess are of less value even though they may have a satisfactory gradient. Eight items were excluded because they were endorsed by more than 10 per cent of the normal population, and these are shown in TABLE 9.

When this had been done 93 items were left: most items had a gradient of response of at least 40, and no item was endorsed by more than 10 per cent of the normal population.

If the responses to item H.1 concerning fatigue are examined (see the end of APPENDIX 4) it can be seen that, although there was some tendency for the more severely ill patients to find the questionnaire very tiring, none the less 81 per cent of all the respondents either found the task 'no bother at all' or thought that, although it was tiring, their responses were accurate. The responses to item H.2 showed that there was a tendency for patients to consider themselves less ill than the doctor looking after them rated them.

At this stage the data was transferred on to punched cards, which entailed punching cards for each of the 300 subjects showing his or her responses to the 93 chosen items, so that the data could be subjected to more elaborate statistical treatment.

TABLE 9

ITEMS REJECTED BECAUSE MORE THAN 10 PER CENT OF 'NORMALS'
ENDORSED THEM

NO.	EXCERPT FROM ITEM	RESPONSE
C. 12	Felt too tired in the evenings to do anything but sit	12–37–56
D. 14	Going out less in the evenings to enjoy yourself	18–51–66
E. 4	Worrying about what is going to happen to your family	22–52–71
E. 12	Felt that others regard you as a touchy person	23–55–57
F. 2	Felt contented with your lot	19–60–69
F. 20	Having a lot of worry over money	19–34–38
F. 22	Feeling easily upset over things	15–52–70
F. 23	Little annoyances upset you	12–49–55

The Principal Components Analysis

Means and standard deviations of the scores for each of the 93 chosen items were computed, and the standard deviations were found to be satisfactory, since the range was from 0·379 to 0·500 with the mode at about 0·470. All the items chosen were found to be highly significant discriminators between the groups, as might have been expected from the selection procedure.

A 93 row by 93 column correlation matrix was then calculated, and a principal components analysis carried out on this matrix. The first factor extracted accounted for no less than 45·6 per cent of the total variance, with the second factor accounting for a mere 3·2 per cent of the total variance. The first 10 factors were examined in some detail, and the items that had high saturations on each factor were examined to see whether they formed meaningful clusters from a psychiatric point of view. It was found that the less the variance that a factor accounted for the less meaningful it appeared to be, and it was eventually decided to consider only the first five factors in the subsequent statistical analysis.

The finding that there is a large general factor accounting for so much of the variance should cause no surprise. Not only were the items selected so that they should each apply to everybody, but the selection procedure after the item analysis was such that specificity has been minimized and generality maximized.

The findings of any principal components analysis are dependent upon the nature of the test items and the population on which the test is calibrated;

with different items or on a different population, other factors might have been obtained.

However, with so much variation concerned with the general factor, and with so little attached to each named factor, it is justifiable to conclude that there is little point in attempting to express 'severity of illness' by a profile of numbers.

It should not be thought that simply because the factors have been given certain names, the factor is what the name says it is. The names that have been tentatively suggested are merely convenient ways of conceptualizing these particular clusters of items.

TABLE 10

THE FIRST FIVE FACTORS FROM THE PRINCIPAL COMPONENTS
ANALYSIS

NUMBER OF THE FACTOR	PERCENTAGE OF THE VARIANCE THAT IT ACCOUNTS FOR	PROVISIONAL DESCRIPTIVE NAME FOR THE BIPOLAR FACTOR
1	45·6	The general factor: 'severity of illness'
2	3·3	Psychic depression versus somatic depression
3	2·6	Agitation versus apathy
4	2·1	Anxiety at night versus anxiety during daytime
5	1·9	Personal neglect versus irritability
	Total 55·5	

The general factor was unique in that every one of the 93 items had high positive loads on it—the lowest factor loadings being 'hands shaking and trembling' with $+0.484$ and 'pains in your head' with $+0.491$. Mathematically, this general factor almost certainly represents the response scale offered for each question ('same as usual', 'less than usual', etc.), and it can therefore be conceptualized as the general way in which the patient perceives that his present state differs from his usual state (Zubin, 1970). Because of this, and from a consideration of the content of the 20 items with the highest factor loadings [see TABLE 11], it has been called 'severity of psychiatric illness'.

The second factor was fairly easy to name, since it was entirely depressive in content, but one end consisted of hypochondriacal, somatic items while the other was entirely psychic, and included the items dealing with suicide. It is shown as TABLE 12.

The third factor was also quite straightforward, since one end consisted of a cluster of items that suggested apathy and retardation, while the other suggested agitation and anxiety [see TABLE 13].

TABLE 11

THE GENERAL FACTOR, 'SEVERITY OF PSYCHIATRIC ILLNESS',
SHOWING THE 20 ITEMS WITH HIGHEST SATURATIONS

EXCERPT FROM ITEM	FACTOR LOADING
Dreading things you have to do	0·808
Felt constantly under strain	0·806
Felt unable to face your problems	0·802
Felt everything on top of you	0·802
Couldn't do anything because your nerves were too bad	0·802
Less capable of making decisions	0·786
Felt scared and panicky for no good reason	0·783
Felt you couldn't overcome your difficulties	0·779
Felt life entirely hopeless	0·775
Felt nervous and strung up all the time	0·772
Feeling life a struggle	0·771
Felt life not worth living	0·770
Thinking of yourself as worthless	0·764
Been losing confidence in yourself	0·763
Can't enjoy normal day-to-day activities	0·759
Losing interest in normal day-to-day activities	0·756
Afraid you might be losing control	0·756
Not able to concentrate on what you're doing	0·750
Wishing you were dead and away from it all	0·747
Lacking energy	0·736

TABLE 12

THE SECOND FACTOR, 'PSYCHIC DEPRESSION VERSUS SOMATIC
DEPRESSION'

	Not feeling well or in good health	+0·387
	Sleep hasn't refreshed you	+0·341
	In need of good tonic	+0·324
SOMATIC	Felt ill	+0·337
DEPRESSION	Run-down and out of sorts	+0·328
	Hot and cold spells	+0·330
	Too tired even to eat	+0·307
	Sweating a lot	+0·301
	versus	
	Idea of taking life kept entering mind	−0·356
	Thought of possibility of making away with yourself	−0·342
PSYCHIC	Wished you were dead and away from it all	−0·305
DEPRESSION	Haven't spent time chatting	−0·291
	Not hopeful about future	−0·255
	Not happy, all things considered	−0·236

TABLE 13

THE THIRD FACTOR, 'AGITATION VERSUS APATHY'

AGITATION	Afraid to say anything in case you made some foolish mistake	+0·322
	Waking early, unable to sleep	+0·296
	Felt that people were looking at you	+0·294
	Losing sleep over worry	+0·288
	Difficulty getting to sleep	+0·284
	Restless and disturbed nights	+0·282
	Unpleasant dreams	+0·254
	versus	
APATHY	Not keeping busy and occupied	−0·310
	Not mentally alert or wide awake	−0·297
	Not able to make a start on anything	−0·296
	Not doing things as well as most others	−0·277
	Getting in late to work	−0·276
	Taking longer over things	−0·253

The fourth factor provides the first real difficulty in conceptualization, since the two clusters do not appear to be the converse of one another. One cluster is fairly homogeneous, and consists of items concerning disturbed sleep. The other cluster consists of anxieties and fears as well as head pains. Both ends seem concerned with anxiety, and they vary mainly according to the time of day or night when one might expect the symptoms—the items are shown as TABLE 14.

TABLE 14

THE FOURTH FACTOR, 'ANXIETY AT NIGHT VERSUS ANXIETY DURING DAYTIME'

ANXIETY AT NIGHT	Difficulty staying asleep at night	+0·507
	Waking early, unable to sleep	+0·490
	Restless and disturbed nights	+0·390
	Difficulty dropping off to sleep	+0·271
	Losing sleep over worry	+0·264
	versus	
ANXIETY DURING DAYTIME	Afraid you might collapse in a public place	−0·265
	Tightness and pressure in head	−0·261
	Pains in the head	−0·270
	Felt people looking at you	−0·245
	Felt scared and panicky for no reason	−0·230
	Afraid to say anything in case you made some foolish mistake	−0·207

Finally, the fifth factor concerns personal feelings, ranging from irritability at one end to personal neglect at the other. It is debatable whether this corresponds to any recognized psychiatric axis, but each cluster considered in isolation is certainly meaningful. It is shown as TABLE 15.

TABLE 15

THE FIFTH FACTOR, 'PERSONAL NEGLECT VERSUS IRRITABILITY'

PERSONAL NEGLECT	Taking less trouble with clothes	+0·341
	Losing interest in appearance	+0·277
	Getting out of house less	+0·259
	versus	
IRRITABILITY	Feeling edgy and bad-tempered	—0·326
	Feeling unhappy and depressed	—0·320
	Taking things hard	—0·304

Preparation of a Shortened Form of the Questionnaire

The principal components analysis was carried out on 93 items, but this was thought to be too great a number of items if the final questionnaire was to achieve its stated aim of being acceptable to a wide range of respondents. Although the principal components analysis had shown that a single general factor accounted for a large proportion of the variance, it still seemed theoretically desirable to retain items that had loadings on the next four factors, since they seemed to correspond to clinically important symptom areas. It was therefore decided to retain all the items that have so far been quoted in TABLES 11 to 15 inclusive: that is to say, the 20 items having the highest loads on the general factor, and 36 other items that had high loads on the next four factors. In addition, three more items were included which were so worded that the mental answer 'yes' indicated health. This was done so that all 18 items of this sort from the 93 items available went through to the final analysis, so that if they were all included it would be possible to produce a final version of the questionnaire 36 items long, that was balanced for 'overall agreement set'. The addition of these three items to the 56 items described above meant that the shortened version of the questionnaire then consisted of 59 items.

Alternative Methods of Scoring the Questionnaire

The GHQ Scoring Method. It will be recalled that this is the scoring method specially devised for the questionnaire, and consists of assigning a score of zero to responses in Columns 1 and 2, and a score of unity to responses in Columns 3 and 4. In the graph in FIGURE 1 the scores of the respondents in each of the three calibration groups are plotted against the proportion of patients in each group having a given score. It can be seen, for example, that 56 per cent of the 'normals', but only 7 per cent of the mildly ill, and none of the severely ill, have a score of zero on the questionnaire. Indeed, the questionnaire emerges as a fairly good discriminator between 'normals' versus 'ills', although less good at discriminating between the various degrees of illness. However, although the scores for the two ill groups are distributed over the entire range, there is a peak for the mildly ill between 0 and 25, and a peak for the severely ill between 45 and 59. Nevertheless, determination of how well the questionnaire discriminates between patients with varying degrees of illness can best be left to later validity studies; at this stage the two ill groups can be combined and called 'cases', and it will then be easier to see which method of scoring achieves the best discrimination between cases and normals.

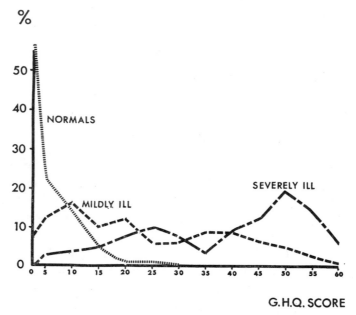

FIG. 1. GHQ Scoring Method (0–0–1–1). Percentage distribution of scores of each of the three calibration groups using the GHQ Scoring Method.

With the GHQ method of scoring the cutting score that gives optimum discrimination between cases and normals is that between 3 and 4, so that respondents with 3 or fewer symptoms are considered normal and those with 4 or more are considered cases. This cutting score gives a total misclassification rate of 13·3 per cent, and if only the cases are considered, 9 per cent of these are misdiagnosed.

These results, using the simplest possible scoring method, may be compared with those obtained with the use of other more elaborate procedures: the Likert scoring methods where different weights are assigned to each column, and using separate weights for each item obtained with a discriminant function analysis.

Likert Scoring Methods. These scoring methods are a way of assigning different scores for different degrees of intensity of response. The simplest

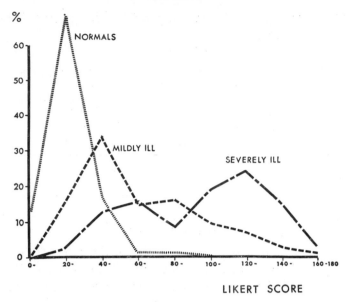

FIG. 2. Simple Likert Scoring Method (0–1–2–3). Percentage distribution of scores of each of the three calibration groups using the Simple Likert Scoring Method.

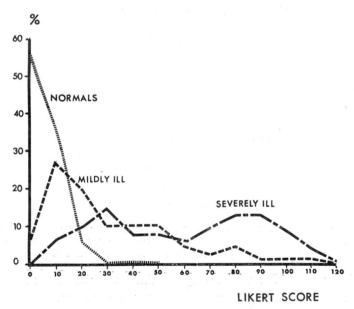

FIG. 3. Modified Likert Scoring Method (0–0–1–2). Percentage distribution of scores of each of the three calibration groups using the Modified Likert Scoring Method.

way of doing this is to assign scores of 0, 1, 2, and 3 to the four response columns reading from left to right. It could, of course, be argued that it is unreasonable to assign any positive score at all to the response 'no more than usual', since this response merely indicates normality. A simple modification of the scoring method would therefore be to assign scores of 0, 0, 1, and 2 to each of the four columns. These two possible scoring methods can be set out as shown in TABLE 16.

TABLE 16

SCORES ASSIGNED TO THE FOUR RESPONSE COLUMNS BY TWO DIFFERENT SCORING METHODS

	COLUMN 1 'Not at all'	COLUMN 2 'No more than usual'	COLUMN 3 'Rather more than usual'	COLUMN 4 'Much more than usual'
SIMPLE LIKERT	0	1	2	3
MODIFIED LIKERT	0	0	1	2

When the questionnaire is scored using the simple Likert scoring method the cutting score that gives optimum discrimination between 'normals' and 'cases' is 39/40: using this, only 12·6 per cent of the 300 subjects, and only 8·5 per cent of the 'cases' are misclassified [FIG. 2]. Using the modified Likert scoring weights and a cutting score of 4/5 the results are not quite so good: 13 per cent of the total population, and 9 per cent of the 'cases', are misclassified [FIG. 3].

The distribution scores for the three calibration groups are shown for each of the three scoring methods described in FIGURES 1, 2, and 3. It can be seen that there is very little to choose between them.

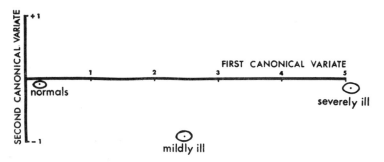

FIG. 4. Results of the Discriminant Function Analysis. Representation of the three groups in two-dimensional space. Each dot represents the mean value for each group, and the ellipse round each dot represents the standard error of the mean.

The Discriminant Function Analysis. This complex statistical analysis enables one to compute weights for each item in such a way that maximum discrimination is obtained between each of the three groups. With *three* calibration groups, it follows that the groups will be maximally separated in *two*-dimensional space (had there been four groups, they would have been separated in three-dimensional space). For technical reasons it was necessary to exclude 10 of the original 59 items initially submitted for the analysis, and the results are shown in FIGURE 4.

The first dimension, or canonical variate, represents the best way of maximally separating the three groups. It accounts for no less than 83·3 per cent of the total variances. It can be conceptualized as a dimension that represents non-specific psychiatric illness, since all of the fairly heterogeneous items used in the analysis contribute to the variation along this dimension.

The second dimension is of great theoretical interest, since it does not distinguish the normals from the severely ill—there is considerable overlap between the standard errors of the means—yet it does discriminate the mildly ill from both the other groups. Examination of the items having the highest loading on this factor shows that the dimension appears to be concerned with gloominess, pessimism and irritability [see TABLE 17]. This dimension accounts for the residual $16\frac{2}{3}$ per cent of the total variance in the analysis.

TABLE 17

ITEMS HAVING HIGH LOADINGS ON THE SECOND DIMENSION

Feeling unhappy and depressed	0·335
Not feeling 'reasonably happy'	0·293
Feeling edgy and bad-tempered	0·292
Not enjoying normal activities	0·280
Feeling unhopeful about the future	0·265

Although this result would not have been predicted, it fits quite well into everyday clinical experience. When the major variance between the three groups has been removed, it is quite meaningful to suppose that this does indeed correspond to the way in which habitual attenders at a psychiatric out-patients' department are different both from acutely disturbed patients on the one hand, and normal patients on the other.

This analysis entailed computing a weight for each item on each dimension, but in the subsequent analysis only the weights on the first dimension are considered, since this is the dimension that discriminates well between the groups. The weights of the various items on this dimension ranged from —0·7 to +0·8.

Scoring the Questionnaire using Weights derived from the Discriminant Function Analysis

The next stage consisted of computing the score of each respondent using the 49 items for which weights were available, so that on this occasion the weights of the items endorsed were summed to obtain the total score. It must be appreciated that this extensive analysis was carried out by the computer—in everyday practice one could only use such precise weights (accurate to five decimal places) if one had a calculating machine.

As might be expected, when these results were plotted graphically the three groups formed three quite distinct peaks with only minimal overlap between them [FIG. 5]. On the other hand, when the new scores were examined from the point of view of case identification, the results were far less impressive.

Using the cutting score of 0·7/0·8 that gave optimum discrimination between 'cases' and 'normals', the total misdiagnosis rate now falls to 11·3 per cent but this entails misclassifying no fewer than 11·5 per cent of the 'cases'. One can, of course, reduce the number of 'cases' that are misclassified by lowering the cutting score, and a cutting score of 0·2/0·3 reduces the number of scores that are missed to 9 per cent, but this is at a cost of a total mis-diagnosis rate of 14·6 per cent.

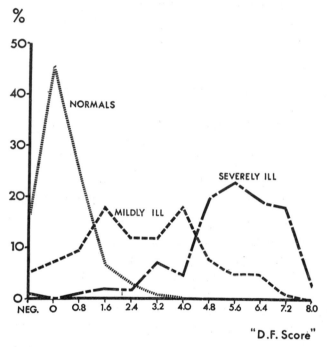

Fig. 5. Discriminant Function Scoring Method (separate weight computed for each item). Percentage distribution of scores of each of the three calibration groups using weights derived from the Discriminant Function Analysis.

CONCLUSION

It is now possible to compare the various scoring methods that might be adopted for the questionnaire from the point of view of case identification. In general terms, 'missing' cases—that is to say, assigning low scores to cases in the present context—is a more severe limitation of a screening test than falsely identifying cases. For this reason both the cutting scores for the discriminant function analysis are set out in TABLE 18, since 11·5 per cent of cases 'missed' is unacceptably high.

The most striking thing about this table is the similarity between the results produced by four very different scoring methods. Of these four methods, the discriminant function analysis is by far the most laborious. If it was to be adopted as the preferred method it would greatly impede the process of scoring each questionnaire. Since it offers no clear advantages over the other methods it will be discarded, and with it the whole notion of assigning separate weights to each item.

Of the two Likert scoring methods, the Modified Likert is inferior to the Simple Likert and may therefore also be discarded, leaving a choice between the GHQ and the Simple Likert scoring methods. The former considers only the number of symptoms and is therefore an 'area' measure, while the latter is a composite measure encompassing both area and intensity. It is interesting, however, that there is relatively little advantage in considering intensity; the overall misclassification rate between cases and normals drops a mere 0·7 per cent when using the more involved scoring method.

TABLE 18

A COMPARISON OF THE RESULTS OBTAINED FROM THE POINT OF VIEW OF CASE IDENTIFICATION OF FOUR DIFFERENT METHODS OF SCORING THE QUESTIONNAIRE

TYPE OF SCORING METHOD	SCORE ASSIGNED TO EACH COLUMN	BEST CUTTING SCORE	TOTAL MISCLASSIFIED %	PERCENTAGE OF 'CASES' MISSED %
DISCRIMINANT FUNCTION ANALYSIS	(separate weight computed for each item)	0·7/0·8	11·3	11·5
		0·2/0·3	14·6	9·0
GHQ SCORE	0–0–1–1	3/4	13·3	9·0
MODIFIED LIKERT	0–0–1–2	4/5	13·0	9·0
SIMPLE LIKERT	0–1–2–3	39/40	12·6	8·5

Since the GHQ scoring method condenses a four-way response scale into a bimodal scale, one might have predicted that the resultant loss of potential information would have made it much less efficient as a scoring method. But as the figures show that it is only marginally less efficient, it must be that the information lost is not very useful from the point of view of case identification. It seems likely that the reasons for this are those set forth in the previous chapter. In the following chapters the two scoring methods will again be compared, both from the point of view of case identification and assessment of the severity of illness.

In the comparison of scoring methods just discussed the analyses were carried out on 59 items selected from the 93 items that were considered in the principal component analysis. The criteria for selection have already been described in detail. The next stage in the development of the questionnaire consisted of printing the selected items so that a shorter, more presentable version of the questionnaire could be used in the assessment studies. Since

59 seemed to be an awkward and rather arbitrary number, an additional item was added to bring the total number of items up to 60. The extra one was, of course, selected from the 24 rejected items from the 93 items mentioned above. It was the item with the steepest gradient in the item analysis of the 24 items.

The resultant 60-item questionnaire can be found in APPENDIX 8. It will be seen that the questions are no longer divided into sections, but as before they start with relatively neutral questions and only gradually lead on to more overtly psychiatric questions.

At this stage, there can be no answer to the question of the best length for the questionnaire. The shorter the questionnaire the more acceptable it becomes, but this is offset by the disadvantage that it must also be less reliable and less valid, since information is discarded as the questionnaire is shortened, and we have shown that all the questions in the 60-item version have discriminatory power. The most rational plan of action would seem to be to use the 60-item questionnaire in the reliability and validity studies to be described in the following chapters, and to find out how much would be lost by shortening the questionnaire in terms of these parameters.

CHAPTER IV

THE ASSESSMENT OF THE PRESENT QUESTIONNAIRE

1. *INTRODUCTION*

ONCE a psychometric instrument has been calibrated on some defined populations, it is necessary to demonstrate that the measurements made are both reliable and valid. If the measures are reliable it implies that the test is measuring some quality in the respondents in a consistent way, and if they are valid it implies that the quality measured bears some relationship to an external variable that is thought to be relevant and important.

There are two main ways of assessing reliability. The first is either to construct parallel versions of the same test, or to divide the test items into two closely comparable subpopulations. Only the latter is appropriate in the present context, and this type of reliability is usually called the *split-half reliability*. The second way of assessing reliability is to administer the test to the same subjects on more than one occasion, and this is called the *test–retest reliability*.

The test–retest reliability of the present questionnaire presents a difficult methodological problem, since the test is meant to assess a potentially highly variable quality in the test subjects. To use an analogy, if one wished to assess the test–retest reliability of a new method for measuring the size of the pupils, it would be necessary to ensure that patients were under conditions of constant illumination on each occasion on which they were assessed. It would, for example, be a powerful criticism of the questionnaire if it were shown to have a high test–retest reliability on a population whose clinical severity *had* in fact altered. It is necessary to show that not only is there a tendency for scores to remain the same if clinical severity does not alter, but also that scores should go up or come down if the patient relapses or improves.

The problem cannot be solved by asking the respondents to complete the questionnaire with a fairly short time interval between tests, since the respondent is being asked to say how he has 'recently' felt about each item. It is clear that if there were only a couple of weeks between the two administrations of the questionnaire, high test–retest reliability figures could be produced merely because on each occasion the respondent was describing the same episode of illness.

Although this problem can be solved by lengthening the interval between the two administrations of the test, the solution itself produces another problem, since it is now necessary to find some way of showing that each patient has remained at about the same degree of clinical disturbance between the two occasions.

The test–retest reliability studies to be reported here will therefore be on patients of whom an independent assessment can be made of their overall degree of disturbance, so that patients who are thought to have stayed about the same can be selected for study. One would expect to find that the more stringent the criteria for deciding that each patient's degree of disturbance has stayed about the same, the higher should be the test–retest reliability. It is conceded that the decision to select patients for the test–retest studies on the basis of an independent assessment of their clinical status is a departure from the usual procedure, since a degree of concurrent validity is implied by the use of such an assessment. In the present context this particular aspect of reliability is, however, of great practical importance, and the split-half coefficients in any case provide a straightforward measure of reliability.

Validity may also be measured in various ways, described in some detail by Cronbach (1949). However, only two of these types of validity—'content validity' and 'concurrent validity'—are relevant to the present questionnaire. Content validity refers to the questionnaire that consists of items whose content is relevant to the variable that one is trying to measure. It is clear that the method used to construct the present questionnaire guarantees that it does have this type of validity.

Concurrent validity refers to the ability of the questionnaire to give scores which are comparable to some external assessment—in this case, judgements about the severity of clinical disturbance made by a psychiatrist at about the same time that the questionnaire was filled in.

Many existing questionnaires and scales—for example, the Beck Depression Inventory, the Zung Scale, and many others—have 'validated' the test by demonstrating that the mean scores for normal controls are significantly lower than the mean scores for a group of identified psychiatric patients. These are really little more than calibration studies: they do not make much demand on the discriminatory power of the scale, since patients with intermediate degrees of disturbance are not included for examination. Of the work reviewed in CHAPTER II, only Macmillan's Health Opinion Survey and Rawnsley's Vale of Glamorgan survey with the Cornell Medical Inventory gave independent clinical and questionnaire assessments to populations containing patients who displayed a whole range of degrees of severity of psychiatric disturbance. Yet, if the questionnaire is to be used as a screening test for psychiatric case identification, it is clear that this is the sort of validation study that must be done. There is therefore little point in conducting a validation study using patients at psychiatric hospitals, since on the one hand they have *all* been identified as psychiatric cases, and on the other the calibration study has already provided a good deal of information concerning these patients.

It is obviously desirable to carry out the validation studies in the sorts of settings in which the questionnaire might eventually be used, and in populations that contain a fair proportion of psychiatrically disturbed patients. It was therefore decided that validity studies should be carried out in a general practice setting and in a medical out-patients' department.

2. *METHOD*

Design of the Test–Retest Reliability Study

The purpose of this study was to compare the scores of a group of patients whose clinical status had not altered over a period of some months. In order to find a population that was likely to contain many patients with longstanding personality disorders and chronic affective illnesses, the questionnaire was given to consecutive patients at the various supportive clinics at the Bethlem Royal and Maudsley Hospitals, excluding patients with schizophrenia, hypomania, or dementia.

The questionnaires were issued to 120 patients between August and December 1967. The questionnaires each had short explanatory letters attached to them, and were handed to the patients by the Registry staff on arrival at the department. They were filled in on tables in the waiting-room and returned to the Registry as each patient left the department. Six months after the first questionnaire had been given out, repeat questionnaires were issued to patients as they came up for their next out-patients' appointment. The patients were asked to compare how they felt on the second occasion with how they had felt on the first, using a simple five-point scale:

1	2	3	4	5
Much worse	Slightly worse	About the same	Slightly better	Much better

It soon became clear that waiting for the patients to come up for another appointment was going to result in long periods of waiting for some individuals, and so after the first 40 of the repeat questionnaires had been collected in this way the remaining 80 questionnaires were posted to the patients in their homes. The obvious disadvantage of this procedure was that while the patients were under the care of the hospital on the first occasion on which the questionnaire was completed, they did not see their doctors on the second occasion, and so the doctors' ratings of change in their mental state were based on inference. In practice this was less important than in theory, since in cases where the doctor was unsure about the patient's clinical status he was allowed to rate them as 'not known'.

When the second questionnaires had all been received, lists were drawn up for each doctor showing the patients that he had seen who were included in this substudy. After each patient's name there appeared three dates: the date on which the patient had completed the questionnaire for the first time and seen the doctor concerned, the date on which the patient completed the questionnaire for the second time, and the date of the patient's appointment with the doctor immediately following the second test administration. The doctors were asked to rate the patients on the same five-point scale that the patients themselves had used [see p. 65].

Some of the doctors concerned could remember the patients sufficiently well to make their ratings from memory, but most of them made their ratings only after examining the patients' notes. Of the 114 patients who filled in pairs of questionnaires, it was possible to collect doctors' ratings in only 87 of them, since in the remainder there had either been a change of doctor, or the patient had been discharged in the meantime.

A Subsidiary Test–Retest Reliability Study

It was realized that the design of the above experiment was not entirely satisfactory, since the ratings by the doctors were being made retrospectively rather than at the time the patients were seen, and the ratings were not being made on the basis of standardized psychiatric assessments. It is, however, surprisingly difficult to collect a large enough group of patients whose clinical status remains unaltered over 6 months.

As will be seen, the validity study in general practice involved seeing a group of 200 surgery attenders who included 96 psychiatric cases; 87 of these psychiatric cases agreed to come up and be seen on a follow-up visit 6 months later, and of these 87 cases 20 were assessed as having the same degree of disturbance on each occasion that they were seen, using a standardized psychiatric assessment on each occasion.

Further details about the standardized psychiatric assessment will be given in the next section: it is sufficient to note here that 174 standardized interviews had to be carried out, each taking 30–60 minutes, in order to collect the 20 pairs of questionnaires. The patient filled in the questionnaire while sitting in the waiting-room before each interview, and the scores were not seen until after the clinical assessments had been made at interview.

One would expect the test–retest reliability figures to be higher in this study than in the larger study in the out-patients' department, since not only was a standardized assessment made of the degree of disturbance on each occasion that the questionnaire was completed, but the assessment was made on the same occasion that the questionnaire was filled in, rather than retrospectively.

Split-half Reliability Study

For this study it was necessary to divide the questionnaire into two equal halves, and to compare the score obtained on one half with the score obtained on the other (Anastasi, 1963). This was done by pairing the items on the basis of their content and the gradients of response to each item found in the item analysis. When this had been done, the first question in each pair was randomly assigned (using random number tables) to either the first or the second half of the questionnaire, with the second question in each pair always being assigned to the remaining half. The purpose of this rather involved process was to ensure that while the items would be randomly assigned to each half, the two halves would be comparable to one another in terms of both ideational content and the discriminatory power of the questions.

This study was carried out on the 853 completed questionnaires that were used in all the other studies reported in this chapter: no group of patients filled in the questionnaire specially for this study.

A Validity Study in General Practice Setting

This validity study was carried out in a suburban general practice which was selected because the general practitioner concerned[1] had extensive research experience and was himself a trained psychiatrist. The validity study of the questionnaire formed part of a more extensive survey into psychiatric illness in general practice which is reported at greater length elsewhere (Goldberg and Blackwell, 1970).

If the questionnaire is to be assessed as a screening test, then it is necessary to make separate assessments of the number of patients who are psychiatrically ill that it misses (its *sensitivity*), and the number of normal patients that it misclassifies as potentially ill (its *specificity*). For this reason it was thought important to see equal numbers of patients with high scores (potential cases) and patients with low scores (potential normals), since it is evident that if the number of patients with high scores had been very small compared with the number of patients with low scores, then the estimate of sensitivity might have been unreliable. It will become clear in the next chapter that if the present results are to be extrapolated to other populations with different prevalences of disorder, separate estimates of sensitivity and specificity are necessary; it seemed desirable to base these estimates on populations of approximately equal sizes. An additional advantage of this arrangement was that all the psychiatrist knew about each patient was that the probability of his having a high score was equal to the probability of his having a low score.

The survey ran from January to June 1968. During this time consecutive attenders at the surgery were asked to fill up the questionnaire while they waited to see the doctor. A notice in the waiting-room explained that a 'Family Health Survey' was taking place, and that all patients were asked to fill in a questionnaire dealing with their recent health. Of 588 different individuals who came up during the survey, completed questionnaires were available for 553. Many of the refusals were for convincing reasons—illiterate, not speaking English, left glasses at home—while only a handful were for unconvincing or odd reasons.

The general practitioner kept a day book during this period, in which he recorded each patient's presenting complaint and his own findings. After he had done this, and just before the patient left, he examined their questionnaire and on the basis of their scores asked them if they would mind seeing another doctor. Very few patients refused this request, and the majority of those who

[1] Dr. B. Blackwell, M.D., D.P.M., General Practitioner, Sanderstead, Surrey; at present Associate Professor of Psychiatry, University of Cincinnati, Ohio, USA.

refused on the grounds that they were in a hurry to get home, came for psychiatric interview the next day. It was the responsibility of the general practitioner to ensure that over the whole period of the survey equal numbers of high scorers and low scorers were sent for psychiatric interview. The patients sent for interview had questionnaire scores drawn from the whole possible range of scores: there was no tendency for very low or very high scorers to be referred. The optimal threshold for case detection in a general practice setting was determined in a 2-week pilot study, and found to be a score of 12 or above to indicate a case.

The main study went on until 200 patients had been interviewed, by which time 553 different patients had completed the questionnaire. The factor that determined whether a patient was asked to stay for interview was that the general practitioner as he went to collect his next patient saw that the door to the interview room was open, thus signifying that the previous interview had been completed. When this happened the next patient seen would be asked to 'see the Family Health Survey doctor', and each patient was introduced to the author by Dr. Blackwell.

The standardized interview schedule used is the *Standardized Psychiatric Interview* of the General Practice Research Unit, described by Goldberg, Cooper, Eastwood, Kedward, and Shepherd (1970). The interview with the patient falls into three sections, while a fourth section of the interview schedule is completed after the patient has left the room. The first section is an unstructured interview with the patient, usually taking only a few minutes, which is used to establish rapport, to discover the reason for the patient's present consultation, and to collect relevant past history.

The second part of the interview is a systematic inquiry into symptoms that the patient may have experienced in the previous week. The symptoms are grouped into 10 areas, beginning with symptoms commonly encountered in everyday life such as headache and fatigue, and only gradually moving towards more obviously psychiatric items such as depression and worry. The interviewer does not ask about florid psychotic phenomena unless he suspects that they are present.

Within each symptom area there are 'mandatory questions' which all patients must be asked, and a series of probes that are asked only if it seems necessary. The interviewer is free to ask any additional questions that seem to be indicated in the particular case he is dealing with, and within each symptom area he aims to establish the frequency and intensity of the particular symptom in the previous week. Simple rules relate frequency and intensity of a symptom to the five-point scale on which each symptom is rated. The third section of the interview is unstructured, and allows the interviewer as much or as little information about the family psychiatric history and the personal history as seems indicated by what has gone before.

After the patient has left, the interviewer assesses the abnormalities that he has seen and heard at the interview, using three scales for abnormalities of behaviour, four for abnormal moods, and five for perceptual and cognitive abnormalities. He therefore makes a total of 22 ratings: 10 ratings of symptoms reported by the patient and 12 ratings of abnormalities manifested at the interview.

TABLE 19

THE 22 RATINGS MADE ON THE BASIS OF THE STANDARDIZED
PSYCHIATRIC INTERVIEW

REPORTED SYMPTOMS	MANIFEST ABNORMALITIES
Somatic symptoms	Slow, lacking spontaneity
Fatigue	Suspicious, defensive
Sleep disturbance	Histrionic
Irritability	Depressed
Lack of concentration	Anxious, agitated, tense
Depression	Elated, euphoric
Anxiety	Flattened, incongruous
Phobias	Depressive thought content
Obsessions and compulsions	Excessive concern with bodily functions
Depersonalization	Thought disorder, delusions, misinterpretations
	Hallucinations
	Intellectual impairment

The detailed criteria for making these five-point ratings, and the definitions of the various abnormal phenomena, have all been gathered together as a 'Manual' which may be consulted when difficult rating problems arise.

The strength of this standardized psychiatric assessment lies in its reliability. This was assessed in a separate study in which six psychiatrists and 40 psychiatric patients took part. Each patient was assessed by two psychiatrists, one of whom acted as interviewer while the other merely observed the interview as co-rater.

An overall reliability coefficient was computed between interviewer and co-rater on the results of a three-way analysis of variance, and separate reliability coefficients were also computed for each reported symptom or manifest abnormality. The results of this study are reported in detail by Goldberg, Cooper, Eastwood, Kedward, and Shepherd (1970). For present purposes it is sufficient to note that the individual reliability coefficients are comparable to those reported for other standardized psychiatric interviews, such as Kendell, Everitt, Cooper, Sartorius, and David (1968), and that the overall reliability coefficient derived from the analysis of variance is $+0.92$.

The patients were each assigned to a position on a six-point rating-scale on the basis of the results of the clinical interview:

0. Not a case: normal, stable individual with or without physical illness.
1. Not a case: subclinical degree of emotional disturbance (includes neurotic personalities without associated affective disturbance).

2. Psychiatric case of mild degree: the psychiatric disturbance is just clinically significant.
3. Psychiatric case of moderate degree.
4. Psychiatric case of marked degree.
5. Psychiatric case of severe degree: should be receiving in-patient care.

A number of observations must be made about this scale. Like the questionnaire itself, it makes the implicit assumption that patients can be arranged along a continuous scale from normality to severe disturbance. This is not a crucial objection to the scale, provided that any resultant correlation between the questionnaire score and the clinical scale is not taken to imply that this underlying assumption has been vindicated. Indeed, by running together categories 0 and 1 ('non-cases') and categories 2, 3, 4, and 5 ('cases') it is possible to convert the clinical assessment into a simple binomial classification that makes no such assumption.

A more serious difficulty concerns the definition of what constitutes a 'clinically significant disturbance' which merits a rating of 2. In the present work the overall rating was derived from the individual ratings in the sense that any patient with a rating of 2 or more in any of the 'manifest abnormalities' section of the clinical schedule was counted as a case. Although this procedure may well have increased the reliability of the overall rating, it in no sense solves the theoretical problem, since a rating of 2 is made only for a manifest abnormality which is present in 'clinically significant' degree. This leaves unanswered the question of what constitutes a 'clinically significant degree of disturbance' for some specified segment of a patient's behaviour and experience.

The question is likely to remain unanswered, since there is no reasonable alternative to adopting the clinical assessments of experienced psychiatrists as the ultimate criteria for case identification. Since this is so, it seemed reasonable to allow the exact position on the six-point scale to be determined partly by the individual ratings made during the semistructured interview, and partly by the overall subjective assessment of the psychiatrist conducting the interview. APPENDIX 5 gives a series of case vignettes to illustrate typical case examples of the various rating positions.

In the course of the 200 interviews genuine difficulty over whether the patient should be rated as 1 (subclinical disturbance) or 2 (psychiatric case: mild) arose in only eight cases. All these patients were eventually classified, although the formulation recorded the essentially arbitrary nature of the decision. The questionnaire scores of this small group of patients were found to be either near or a little above the adopted threshold.

A Validity Study in the Medical Out-patients' Department of a General Hospital

This validity study formed part of a survey of psychiatric aspects of diseases of the small intestine, that was carried out in the Medical Out-patients'

Department of St. Thomas's Hospital between August 1967 and August 1968. The 91 patients consisted of 46 with idiopathic steatorrhea, 23 with Crohn's disease, 11 with alactasia, and the remainder with miscellaneous conditions such as post-vagotomy state, pancreatic steatorrhea, and small bowel diarrhoea.

All patients known to the department as having conditions affecting their small intestine were seen in the survey, and each patient was interviewed after being examined by the physician who usually attended him. The patients were again not told that the author was a psychiatrist, but only that the consultant in charge of their case had asked him to carry out a systematic survey on all patients with their particular condition. The interview began with a short medical history, but then went on to the same semistructured psychiatric interview that was used in the validity study in general practice. As before, each interview took between half an hour and an hour.

At the end of the interview the patient was given the present questionnaire and the Middlesex Hospital Questionnaire (Crown and Crisp, 1966) to take home with him, together with a stamped addressed envelope. Most patients returned their questionnaires within a few days, and the few that forgot to do so were reassessed at a subsequent attendance and asked to fill in another questionnaire. The findings of this survey relating specifically to the relationship between psychiatric disturbance and diseases of the small intestine are reported at length elsewhere (Goldberg, 1970).

3. RESULTS

Results with the 60-item Questionnaire

Test–Retest Reliability. The questionnaires of the 114 out-patients who had filled in pairs of questionnaires revealed that although they had all completed the questionnaire, less than half of them had filled in the separate rating-scale comparing how they felt on the two occasions. Of these patients only 19 indicated that they felt 'about the same'. However, it was also possible to make an estimate of how the patient felt on the two occasions by examining the five-point global self-rating that the patients made about themselves at the end of the questionnaire, in answer to the question, 'Do you feel that you are at all ill?'

In the whole group of 114 patients 65 thought that they had stayed about the same, a figure that was arrived at by adding patients with identical self-ratings on each occasion to the 19 patients who had remembered to fill in the comparative self-rating, and had rated themselves 'about the same'. In contrast, 24 patients thought that they had improved, 15 that they had deteriorated, while 10 gave inconsistent responses, or no responses, to these self-ratings.

Because of changes in medical staff and the fact that several of the patients had either been discharged or had failed to reattend, although they had sent back the questionnaires, medical assessments of change could only be obtained for 87 patients. Of these, 51 were rated as about the same, 21 were rated as slightly better, 7 as definitely better, 7 as slightly worse, and 1 as definitely worse.

In addition to the test–retest study in the out-patients' department, it will be recalled that a small series of 20 patients seen by the author at a 6-month follow-up in the general practice validity study were also included as a small subsidiary test–retest study, with the expectation that since the criteria for the patient's having remained approximately the same were far more stringent in this study, the test–retest reliability coefficient should be higher. TABLE 20 shows that this prediction has been fulfilled.

TABLE 20

TEST–RETEST RELIABILITY COEFFICIENT ON THREE GROUPS OF PATIENTS WHO COMPLETED THE GENERAL HEALTH QUESTIONNAIRE ON TWO OCCASIONS 6 MONTHS APART

GROUP	NUMBER	RELIABILITY COEFFICIENT
Patients given standardized psychiatric interview by author on each occasion	20	+0·90
Patients who in their opinion stayed about the same	65	+0·75
Patients who in their doctors' opinion stayed about the same	51	+0·51

Split-half Reliability. This was computed for all the 853 questionnaires available, and was found to be +0·95.

General Practice Validity Study

When the 200 clinical interviews had been completed the patients' questionnaires were scored by transferring the responses on to punched cards. The more accurate scoring procedure revealed that the general practitioner had in fact sent in 102 high scorers and 98 low scorers over the 5 months of the survey. If the patients' scores on the questionnaire are plotted against the overall clinical assessment, the results can be seen in FIGURE 6 [see p. 73]. (No patients were thought to be so disturbed as to require in-patient treatment, and so rating position 5 is not shown.)

The product-moment correlation between questionnaire score and overall clinical assessment has been computed and found to be +0·80. These results may be shown in a more simple way by dividing the questionnaire results into 'potential cases' (scores of 12 or above) and 'potential normals' (scores of 11 or below), and by dividing the clinical assessments into 'normals' (0 and 1) and 'cases' (2, 3, and 4). This gives four categories of respondents, as in TABLE 21.

This table shows that 183 patients—91·5 per cent—were correctly identified by the questionnaire, and only 8·5 per cent were misclassified. An overall

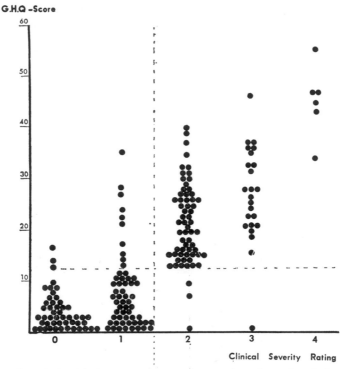

FIG. 6. The relationship between score on the questionnaire and an independent standardized psychiatric assessment of the severity of psychiatric disturbance for 200 general practice patients.

TABLE 21

THE RELATIONSHIP BETWEEN QUESTIONNAIRE SCORES AND CLINICAL ASSESSMENTS FOR THE 200 PATIENTS

Potential Cases (scores 12 and over on questionnaire)	FALSE POSITIVES $n = 13$	TRUE POSITIVES $n = 89$
Potential Normals (scores 11 and below on questionnaire)	TRUE NEGATIVES $n = 94$	FALSE NEGATIVES $n = 4$
	Normals at interview	Psychiatric cases at interview
	PSYCHIATRIC ASSESSMENT	

misclassification rate is insufficiently informative, however, since it is itself dependent upon the prevalence of the disease in the population in question; it is of greater interest to calculate 'sensitivity' and 'specificity' separately. Sensitivity is calculated by expressing the 'true positives' as a percentage of all psychiatric cases found at interview, and specificity is calculated by expressing the number of 'true negatives' as a percentage of the total number of non-cases. The present figures of 95·7 per cent for sensitivity and 87·8 per cent for specificity are very satisfactory, and indeed compare favourably with those quoted for other screening tests in medicine (Wilson and Jungner, 1968).

Since the 200 patients in this study were intensively studied, it is of interest to examine the 'false positives' and 'false negatives' in an attempt to investigate the possible determinants of misclassification. One possibility is that some of the 'false positives' may have had high scores because of physical rather than

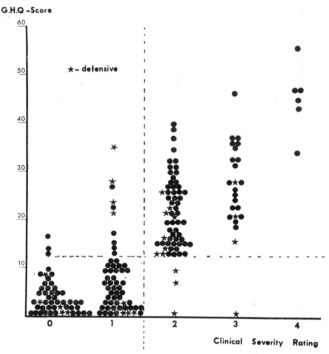

FIG. 7. The relationship between score on the questionnaire and an independent clinical psychiatric assessment for 200 general practice patients, showing those patients who were thought to be 'defensive' at the interview.

psychiatric illness. When the schedules of the 13 'false positives' were examined, five of them were found to be physically ill, but physical illness was also common among the 'true negatives'. One way of dealing with this problem is to carry out a special item analysis on patients thought to have an 'entirely physical illness', and to try the effect of removing those items that tend to be answered positively by the physically ill. This will be done in the next section, when shortened versions of the questionnaire are considered.

Another way of considering the misclassified respondents is to assume that their responses are inconsistent: either they are prepared to admit in a face-to-face situation what they will not admit on paper ('false negatives'), or they claim more symptoms on paper than they later admit at interview ('false positives'). Such behaviour could be thought of as defensive. It will be recalled that one of the 12 manifest abnormalities that was recorded at interview was 'suspicious, defensive', and that the patients were rated on this well before their questionnaire scores were known. Patients were rated as defensive either on the basis of their manner and behaviour, or because of remarks like, 'Can I be sure that this is absolutely confidential?'. It is of interest to examine the relationship between defensiveness in the interview situation and the tendency to give inconsistent responses on the questionnaire and at interview. In FIGURE 7 patients who manifested defensiveness at interview have been depicted by a star rather than a dot [see p. 74].

It can be seen that all the 'false negatives' and nearly a third of the 'false positives' were thought to be defensive, and it therefore seems likely that the sort of defensiveness that can be assessed at interview is related to misclassification of respondents by the questionnaire.

The Validity Study in a Medical Out-patients' Department

The results of the validity study at St. Thomas's Hospital are broadly comparable to those found in general practice, and are shown in FIGURE 8 [see p. 76].

It can be seen that there is a tendency for patients in this setting to have lower scores, and that there are relatively more false negatives and fewer false positives than in a general practice setting. This is probably because most of these patients had been attending the department for some years, so that their illnesses tended to be more chronic than those seen in general practice. To some extent this tendency can be remedied by adopting a lower threshold score, and in TABLE 22 the various figures are given both for the general practice threshold (11/12) and a slightly lower threshold (9/10).

TABLE 22

VALIDITY DATA ON THE GENERAL HEALTH QUESTIONNAIRE IN A MEDICAL OUT-PATIENTS' DEPARTMENT ON 91 PATIENTS USING THE SAME THRESHOLD SCORE THAT WAS ADOPTED FOR A GENERAL PRACTICE SETTING (11/12) AND A SLIGHTLY LOWER THRESHOLD (9/10)

	THRESHOLD SCORE	
	9/10	11/12
Correlation between GHQ score and psychiatric assessment	+0·77	+0·77
Overall misclassification rate	8·8%	10·9%
Sensitivity	87·1%	80·6%
Specificity	93·3%	93·3%

These figures are broadly similar to those found in a general practice setting, and it is submitted that they indicate that the questionnaire is of acceptable validity both as a case identifier and as an indicator of the severity of psychiatric disturbance in both these settings.

The Scores of Patients whose Clinical State Alters

Since the questionnaire is meant to indicate severity of psychiatric disturbance at the time of its completion, it is necessary to show that not only do the scores of patients remain the same if the patients' clinical statuses remain

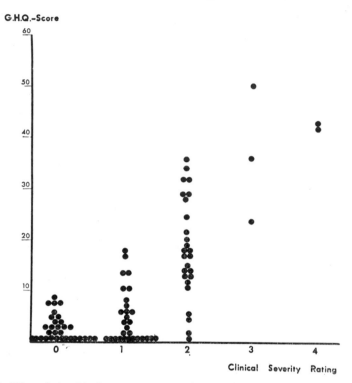

FIG. 8. The relationship between score on the questionnaire and an independent standardized psychiatric assessment of the severity of psychiatric disturbance for 91 patients in a medical out-patients' department of a general hospital.

constant, but that scores will go down if patients improve, and go up if they deteriorate. There is good reason to suppose that this is the case.

In the test–retest reliability study described earlier in the chapter some patients thought that they had improved and others that they had deteriorated, when they filled in the questionnaire on the second occasion. The relationship of their scores to their self-assessments is explored in TABLE 23.

This table confirms that a given patient's score comes down or goes up depending on whether, in his opinion, he gets better or worse. It will be recalled that in the 'subsidiary test–retest study' described earlier, 87 patients agreed to come back for reassessment 6 months after their first assessment, and in addition to the questionnaire each patient was interviewed by the author using the standardized clinical interview. Since all the patients were

TABLE 23

THE EFFECT OF OVERALL IMPROVEMENT OR DETERIORATION
ON THE MEAN GHQ SCORE

	NUMBER	MEAN SCORE ON IST OCCASION	MEAN SCORE ON 2ND OCCASION	DIFFERENCE	STANDARD ERROR OF DIFFERENCE
Patients who had IMPROVED	24	20·0	2·29	17·61[1]	3·51
Patients who had STAYED THE SAME	55	9·84	10·98	1·14[NS]	1·39
Patients who had DETERIORATED	15	15·66	35·06	19·40[1]	4·21

[1] $P > 0.001$.

TABLE 24

THE RELATIONSHIP OF AN INDEPENDENT CLINICAL ASSESSMENT
OF CHANGE TO THE MEAN GHQ SCORE

	NUMBER	MEAN SCORE ON IST OCCASION	MEAN SCORE ON 2ND OCCASION	DIFFERENCE	STANDARD ERROR OF DIFFERENCE
Patients who GREATLY IMPROVED	37	25·05	2·00	23·05[1]	1·88
Patients who SLIGHTLY IMPROVED	24	19·79	6·25	13·54[1]	2·02
Patients who REMAINED THE SAME	20	18·85	14·90	3·95	2·90
Patients who GOT SLIGHTLY WORSE	6	22·33	31·00	8·66[NS]	3·80

[1] $P > 0.001$.

disturbed at their initial assessment, it is not surprising that the overall tendency was to improve [see TABLE 24].

In addition to these data, in the general practice validity study the general practitioner also administered the questionnaire to a number of patients whose clinical severity seemed to him to have altered since they completed the questionnaire on their index consultation. Although the numbers are relatively small, they are included here because they provide information about patients who had deteriorated, as well as those who had improved [see TABLE 25].

The figures quoted in this section show that scores on the questionnaire not only remain constant in patients whose clinical severity remains the same, but also go up if patients deteriorate and come down if they improve.

TABLE 25

THE RELATIONSHIP OF THE GENERAL PRACTITIONER'S CLINICAL ASSESSMENT TO CHANGE IN THE MEAN GHQ SCORE

	NUMBER	MEAN SCORE ON 1ST OCCASION	MEAN SCORE ON 2ND OCCASION	DIFFERENCE	STANDARD ERROR OF DIFFERENCE
Patients who had IMPROVED	14	31·5	7·6	23·8[1]	3·24
Patients who had DETERIORATED	7	6·71	25·4	18·7[1]	3·43

[1] $P > 0.001$.

Shortened Versions of the Questionnaire

It will be recalled that at the end of CHAPTER III the need to compute reliability and validity coefficients for the 60-question questionnaire, and to find out how much would be lost by shortening the questionnaire, was mentioned. In general terms, as the questionnaire becomes shorter it is likely to be refused by fewer respondents and to take less time to complete, but as information is being discarded it is likely to become less reliable and less valid.

There are various ways of shortening the questionnaire, and these will be considered in turn.

First, one could construct a questionnaire that was balanced in terms of 'overall agreement set', in that half the propositions would indicate health if answered 'yes', while the remainder would indicate illness. There are 18 questions in the 60-item questionnaire where 'yes' indicates health, as opposed to 42 questions where 'yes' indicates illness. The first shortened version of the questionnaire was prepared by selecting the 18 best questions from these 42 questions and combining them with the 18 questions to which 'yes' indicated health. They were the 'best' in the sense that they had the steepest gradients in the item analysis.

Secondly, a questionnaire could be constructed where the only criterion of item selection was the steepness of the gradients in the item analysis. In order to allow a meaningful comparison with the first method of shortening, this was done so that the 36 'best' items were selected from the 60 items.

Finally, an allowance could be made for physical illness, since it had already been found in the validity study in general practice that some 'false positives' occurred who were physically rather than psychiatrically ill. Obviously someone with, say, lobar pneumonia might well give positive replies to items like, 'Have you recently felt that you are ill?', and 'Have you recently been feeling run-down and out of sorts?', without this indicating psychiatric disturbance.

It was possible to find which items tended to be answered positively by physically ill patients by carrying out a new item analysis on the questionnaire. It will be recalled that 553 patients filled in the questionnaire while waiting to see the general practitioner. Of these, 252 were diagnosed by him as suffering from an 'entirely physical illness'. When an item analysis was carried out on the questionnaires of this group of patients it was possible to identify a group of questions that were answered 'yes' by more than 12 per cent of the patients. These questions are listed in TABLE 26.

TABLE 26

THE QUESTIONS ANSWERED POSITIVELY BY MORE THAN 12 PER CENT OF THE PATIENTS WITH 'ENTIRELY PHYSICAL ILLNESS'

HAVE YOU RECENTLY
— been feeling perfectly well and in good health?
— been feeling in need of a good tonic?
— been feeling run-down and out of sorts?
— felt that you are ill?
— been getting any pains in your head?
— been getting up feeling that your sleep hasn't refreshed you?
— been feeling mentally alert and wide awake?
— been feeling full of energy?
— had difficulty in getting off to sleep?
— been taking longer over the things that you do?
— been getting out of the house as much as usual?
— been getting edgy and bad-tempered?

The third shortened version of the questionnaire was therefore prepared by excluding these items, and then selecting the 36 items with the steepest gradients from the *original* item analysis. When this has been done the three versions of the questionnaire could be compared from the point of view both of their reliability and of validity coefficients, and from their use in case identification. These figures are shown in TABLE 27.

From the point of view of reliability and validity coefficients little is lost by shortening the questionnaire by any of the three ways, but from the point of view of case identification the 'overall agreement set' is better than either of the other two methods, mainly because its specificity is superior to theirs.

It therefore seemed reasonable to try three further degrees of shortening the questionnaire—to 30, 20, and 12 items respectively. All these selections were 'balanced' for overall agreement set, all were carried out with 'physical illness' questions (listed in TABLE 26) excluded, and all were carried out using the items with the steepest gradients from the original item analysis after these two preliminary steps had been taken. For ease of comparison the results for all these versions of the questionnaire have been gathered together as TABLE 27, and the actual items that were used in each version of the questionnaire are listed in APPENDIX 6.

TABLE 27

RELIABILITY AND VALIDITY COEFFICIENTS, AND DATA RELEVANT TO CASE IDENTIFICATION, FOR PROGRESSIVELY SHORTER VERSIONS OF THE QUESTIONNAIRE USING THE GHQ SCORING METHOD, AND SHOWING THE EFFECTS OF USING THE LIKERT SCORING METHOD FOR THE 60-ITEM VERSION OF THE QUESTIONNAIRE

	RELIABILITY			VALIDITY		Cutting score	OVERALL MISCLASSIFICATION RATE		SENSITIVITY		SPECIFICITY	
	Test retest (Pts.)	Test retest (Drs.)	Split half	GP	STH		GP %	STH %	GP %	STH %	GP %	STH %
GHQ SCORE												
60 Items	0·76	0·51	0·95	0·80	0·77	11/12	8·5	10·9	95·7	80·6	87·8	93·3
36 Items ('BEST')	0·75	0·50	0·94	0·79	0·77	6/7	12·5	9·8	95·7	83·9	80·4	93·3
36 Items ('OAS')	0·76	0·54	0·92	0·81	0·76	7/8	10·0	13·2	92·5	67·7	87·8	96·7
36 Items (Physically ill)	0·78	0·52	0·93	0·79	0·74	4/5	12·0	13·2	94·6	77·4	82·2	91·6
30 Items	0·77	0·53	0·92	0·80	0·72	4/5	11·0	14·3	91·4	64·5	87·0	91·6
20 Items	0·73	0·49	0·90	0·77	0·72	3/4	13·0	14·3	88·2	64·5	86·0	96·7
12 Items	0·73	0·52	0·83	0·77	0·72	1/2	14·5	12·1	93·5	74·2	78·5	95·0
LIKERT SCORING												
60 Items	0·75	0·58	0·96	0·78	0·76	46/47	14·0	15·4	92·5	77·5	80·4	88·4

The reliability and validity coefficients listed in TABLE 27 show a gradual fall with progressively shorter versions of the questionnaire, as had been expected, although even at a length of only 12 items they are still surprisingly high. From the point of view of case identification the increase in overall misclassification is rather more marked, but it is encouraging to note that at only half its present length (i.e. at 30 items) it still correctly classifies 89 per cent of the general practice patients and 85·7 per cent of the medical out-patients.

A Final Comparison of the GHQ and Likert Scoring Methods

At the end of CHAPTER III the GHQ method of scoring was shown to produce fairly similar results to the Likert scoring method when the results of the calibration groups were considered, and it was decided to repeat the comparison between these two scoring methods with the reliability and validity data.

Only the Simple Likert scoring method, where the four columns are assigned weights of 0, 1, 2, and 3 respectively, was used for the purposes of this comparison, since this method was found to be superior to the Modified Likert (0, 0, 1, 2) method [see CHAPTER III]. The results of using the Likert method of scoring are shown as the bottom row of results in TABLE 27.

Of the five reliability and validity coefficients, two are slightly better and three are slightly worse if the Likert method is used. For case identification, the results with the Likert method are undoubtedly inferior to those obtained with the GHQ method.

Finally, it must be remembered that of the two scoring methods the GHQ method is by far the least trouble, since the person scoring the questionnaire has only to make a quick count of responses in the right-hand columns. This usually takes little more than 10 seconds. On the other hand, the Likert method involves pencil and paper, or a series of 60 consecutive addition sums. Since the method gives results that are if anything inferior to the GHQ method, it will not be considered further.

A Validity Study in the United States

Further validity studies were carried out during a sabbatical year spent at the University of Pennsylvania in Philadelphia. These were undertaken, in collaboration with Dr. Karl Rickels of the Psychopharmacology Research Unit, in the practices of five general practitioners who had previously co-operated with research projects.

In each practice the design was broadly similar to that already described in Dr. Blackwell's practice, except that the patients were asked to complete two questionnaires while they waited to see the doctor: the 30-item General Health Questionnaire [see APPENDIX 6] and the 36-item Symptom Checklist (SCL) already described in CHAPTER II. The item content of the SCL is broadly comparable to that of the GHQ, but each item is scored on a four-point frequency scale: Not at all—a little—quite a bit—extremely.

This extra validity survey had four objectives:

1. To test the effectiveness of a 30-item version of the questionnaire. (The data reported for a 30-item questionnaire in TABLE 27 were based on the 60-item questionnaire, and calculated by considering only the responses to the '30 best' items.)
2. To measure the effectiveness of the questionnaire in a different cultural setting and in a number of different practices.
3. To discover the effects of race and social class on mean GHQ scores. (All the respondents in London had been white, and the sample was skewed in favour of upper social classes.)
4. To compare the effectiveness of the GHQ as a screening test with the SCL when each test was used on the same population and measured against the same criterion assessment.

The five practices were all in the Greater Philadelphia area, and were chosen in such a way that a wide range of social classes would be represented, and at least 100 of the 250 respondents would be black. In each practice, consecutive attenders completed the questionnaires and handed them to the receptionist, and the author then interviewed patients selected by the general practitioner until 50 interviews had been completed. Since all the doctors concerned were in private practice they had to be allowed to use their own discretion about whom to send in for an interview. They were told not to look at the questionnaire and to send patients in for interview whether or not they considered them to be 'cases'. As things turned out the doctors usually sent their next patient in for an interview whenever the author told the receptionist that he was free, but they also often asked patients to wait and see the author when they considered them to be 'cases'. In one practice in the 'ghetto' area many patients were illiterate, and in these cases a research assistant read the questions out to the patients.

When the scores in each questionnaire were plotted against standardized clinical assessment, each correlated with it well (product-moment correlation for GHQ $= +0.77$), but the GHQ was superior to the SCL as a screening test because there were fewer false positives associated with its use. Many patients who at interview struck the author as being neurotic personalities, but who were *not* ill, endorsed 'same as usual' on the GHQ and therefore appeared as true negatives, but endorsed 'a little' on the SCL and therefore appeared as false positives. The sensitivity and specificity found for each questionnaire are shown in TABLE 28, and the overall misclassification rate is based on a population with a prevalence of 25 per cent.

When these figures for the general health questionnaire are compared with those predicted for a 30-item questionnaire in TABLE 27 they are considerably less good, presumably mainly because the American population was very different from the populations used to calibrate the test. Nevertheless, it still performs better as a screening test than the Symptom Checklist despite the fact that the latter is an American test. In view of the broad similarity in item content this must mainly be due to the form of the response scale used in each test. Other aspects of the survey are reported elsewhere (Rickels, Goldberg, and Hesbacher, 1972), and the effects of major demographic variables on mean score are given in APPENDIX 7.

TABLE 28

A COMPARISON OF THE 30-ITEM GENERAL HEALTH QUESTIONNAIRE WITH THE SYMPTOM CHECKLIST AS SCREENING TESTS ON 247 PATIENTS ATTENDING GENERAL PRACTITIONERS IN PHILADELPHIA

	CUTTING SCORE	SENSITIVITY %	SPECIFICITY %	OVERALL MISCLASSIFICATION (at 25 per cent prevalence) %
General Health Questionnaire (30 items)	3/4	85	79·5	19·1
Symptom Checklist (36 items)	14/15	84	68·8	27·4

4. CONCLUSION

The salient point in the complex array of data presented in TABLE 27 is that no version of the questionnaire is as good as the 60-item questionnaire scored by the GHQ method. At this length the questionnaire has been found acceptable to well over 90 per cent of potential respondents. Whether shortening the questionnaire would necessarily make it more acceptable to potential respondents is not clear, but one would expect it to do so to some extent. In deciding to use a shorter version of the questionnaire, the research worker must weigh the advantages of gaining a few more respondents against the certain loss of information that the use of a shorter version would entail.

Where there is reason to believe that the population on which the questionnaire is to be used is well disposed towards either the survey itself or the person carrying it out, there would seem to be no point in using a shorter version of the questionnaire, and it should be used at its present length. If, on the other hand, there is reason to suppose that these conditions do not obtain, or if for some reasons peculiar to the projected survey it is not possible to use the 60-item questionnaire, then the 30-item questionnaire could be used instead.

Whichever version of the questionnaire is decided upon for a particular survey, the data shown in TABLE 27 will enable the investigator to look up the reliability and validity data of the instrument he has chosen to use.

CHAPTER V

DISCUSSION

In no department of medical inquiry, probably, has there been manifest so little of the truly scientific spirit as in the statistics of insanity. The plainest rules of philosophical investigation have been disregarded, things have been associated having no necessary relation, and conclusions drawn that had but an indifferent foundation in facts. . . . When we undertake to give a numerical value to such events as the causes of the disease, the date of its origin, the number of recoveries, &c., we are dealing with the uncertain and the indefinite, differently interpreted by different persons. What we record on these points might greatly differ from the records of other observers, and thus it may be worse than useless as a matter of statistics. And this objection must lie against every incident the meaning of which can be open to doubt, or diversity of opinion.

Isaac Ray, Boston, 1873

WHEN Isaac Ray wrote these words it was not possible to make realistic assessments even of the numbers of patients with major psychiatric illnesses who existed in the community. The advent of modern survey methods described in CHAPTER II has meant that there is now broad agreement about the prevalence rates for major psychiatric illnesses in various communities, but it is still true to say that widely varying estimates have been made of the prevalence of neurotic illnesses. It has been shown that these wide variations depend in large part upon differences in survey methods adopted by research teams.

In CHAPTER I it was stated that the aim of the present work was to produce a self-administered questionnaire that would identify respondents with a non-psychotic psychiatric illness by making an assessment of the severity of their psychiatric disturbance. The questionnaire was to be easy to administer, acceptable to respondents, fairly short, and objective in the sense that it would not require the person administering it to make any subjective assessments about the respondent. It is now possible to examine the extent to which these aims have been realized.

The questionnaire has been given to well over 6000 respondents in a wide variety of settings, and in over 650 cases the questionnaire has been followed by a standardized psychiatric interview with the author. It has usually been administered by lay workers such as receptionists and nurses, and the requirements for successful administration seem to be only that the respondent should have 10–15 minutes of spare time and a table and chair. When administered by a receptionist the questionnaire was found to be acceptable to just under 95 per cent of consecutive attenders in a suburban general practice, and when patients were asked to complete the questionnaire by a doctor refusals were very unusual. As shown in the previous chapter, even if the questionnaire is reduced to as few as 30 questions the reliability and validity coefficients do not greatly alter, although the questionnaire is slightly less satisfactory for case identification. Since the questionnaire is self-administered with an objective scoring method it is in no way dependent upon what Ray termed 'the different interpretations by different persons', and the standardized psychiatric interview which has been used to validate the questionnaire has been shown to have a high reliability when used by different psychiatrists.

RESPONSE SETS

One of the claims to originality of the present work is that considerable attention has been given to the problems of the response sets which may affect responses to questionnaires. Since the GHQ method has been found to be the most satisfactory of the four different methods of scoring the questionnaire that were tried, it is worth recalling that this method eliminates the error of central tendency and the problems associated with Likert scales, while greatly reducing the bias associated with bimodal response scales. The problem of overall agreement set has been partly solved by the form of the response scale adopted, and the shorter versions of the questionnaire given in APPENDIX 6 are balanced for overall agreement set.

The Problem of 'Social Desirability' (SD)

The response set that could not be reduced was 'social desirability', since it was difficult to think of any way of asking about psychiatric symptoms that eliminated this source of error.

If it was an important source of error, we should expect that people who had high SD scores would not be prepared to admit to psychiatric symptoms on the questionnaire. Since no one would expect having a high SD score to give a patient immunity from psychiatric illness, the complete prediction would be that persons with high SD scores should appear as true negatives (if they were not in fact cases) or as false negatives (if they were cases). The addition of such patients with high SD scores to the true and false negatives would be expected to increase the mean SD score of these two groups.

In order to investigate this hypothesis, Crowne and Marlow's SD scale, together with the Eysenck Personality Inventory, were collected from 70 'true positives', 9 'false positives', and 9 'false negatives', as well as a group of 30 'true negatives' who had been diagnosed by the author as 'entirely physical illness' at the standardized psychiatric interview. The results are shown in TABLE 29.

It can be seen from this table that the hypothesis is not confirmed, and 'social desirability' emerges as a relatively unimportant determinant of responses on this questionnaire, despite its obvious potential theoretical significance.

The results of the Eysenck Personality Inventory are shown in TABLE 30. (E = extroversion score; N = neuroticism score; L = lie score.)

TABLE 29

THE RELATIONSHIP OF THE 'SOCIAL DESIRABILITY' SCORE TO
THE GHQ SCORE AND THE RESULTS OF INTERVIEW

HIGH SCORES ON GHQ (12 or more)	FALSE POSITIVES $n = 9$ Mean SD Score = 18·4 Standard Dev. = 5·02	TRUE POSITIVES $n = 70$ Mean SD Score = 18·0 Standard Dev. = 5·83
LOW SCORES ON GHQ (11 or fewer)	TRUE NEGATIVES $n = 30$ Mean SD Score = 20·3 Standard Dev. = 4·57	FALSE NEGATIVES $n = 9$ Mean SD Score = 18·0 Standard Dev. = 6·0
	Non-cases at interview	Psychiatric cases at interview

TABLE 30

THE RELATIONSHIP OF THE EYSENCK PERSONALITY INVENTORY
SCORES TO THE GHQ SCORE AND THE RESULTS OF INTERVIEW

HIGH SCORES ON GHQ	FALSE POSITIVES $n = 9$ E = 10·9 N = 7·3 L = 4·0	TRUE POSITIVES $n = 70$ E = 11·7 N = 11·3 L = 3·5
LOW SCORES ON GHQ	TRUE NEGATIVES $n = 30$ E = 12·7 N = 8·4 L = 2·6	FALSE NEGATIVES $n = 9$ E = 10·9 N = 11·8 L = 2·2
	Non-cases at interview	Psychiatric cases at interview

It is interesting to see that the 'cases' had high mean neuroticism scores irrespective of their scores on the general health questionnaire, and also that there is a tendency for high scorers on the general health questionnaire to have high 'lie scores'. This seems particularly true of the 'false positives', but the numbers are small.

The latter finding is especially difficult to interpret, since the naïve assumption that patients with high GHQ scores are liars is contradicted by the fact that the GHQ score has been shown to furnish reliable and valid information about present psychiatric disturbance. It is worth noting that Eysenck has in any case never demonstrated that respondents with high L scores are liars; he has merely assumed that they are from a consideration of the content of the items. Yet, in fact, there are a number of alternative explanations, of which one is that the tendency to have a high L score is at least partly determined by emotional instability at the time the questionnaire is completed.

In conclusion, it is interesting to observe that despite the polemics among psychologists concerning the importance of response sets (Rorer, 1965; Jackson, 1967), they have been shown to be relatively trivial determinants of response in the particular psychometric task with which this monograph has been concerned. This statement requires some qualification in the case of overall agreement set, since the design of the questionnaire is such that the effects of agreement set have been minimized, and there are minor advantages in using a questionnaire that is 'balanced' for agreement set. In the case of 'end-users' versus 'middle-users', the advantages gained by correcting for this source of error with the GHQ scoring method are almost balanced by the information lost by discarding the weighted scores used by the Likert scoring methods. It is interesting to note that what is in effect a mere overall count of symptoms (the GHQ method) gives results which are if anything better than the more complex Likert method, which allows for both the intensity *and* number of the symptoms to contribute to the total score, since this replicates Kellner's findings described in CHAPTER II. It is certainly fortunate that the one response set that could not be eliminated from the questionnaire—social desirability—does not seem to be very important in this particular context.

It follows from what has been said that such strengths as the questionnaire possesses as a case identifier can only be partly due to the attention that was paid to the effects of response sets. The rest of the explanation must lie in the distinction between symptoms of illness and personality traits made by the method adopted for the layout of each item, and the fact that the questionnaire was calibrated on a similar population to that in which the reliability and validity studies were carried out, with careful item selection by means of the item analysis.

TWO WAYS OF CONCEPTUALIZING A SCORE ON THE QUESTIONNAIRE

An assumption that has so far run through the present work has been that non-psychotic psychiatric disturbance is distributed throughout the population in varying degrees of severity, so that one may postulate an axis running from severe disturbance to a hypothetical normality. The questionnaire is thought to be measuring along such an axis, so that a given respondent is assigned a position on the axis to known limits of error. This error is itself determined partly by such shortcomings as are peculiar to this questionnaire and partly by limitations that are inherent in the use of any questionnaire: namely, that it is based on what the subject is prepared to admit on paper rather than on direct observation of morbid phenomena. The results of the principal components analysis given in CHAPTER III did not support the idea that it was necessary to give a profile of scores on different dimensions of severity of disturbance. Viewed in this way, then, a respondent's score can be thought of as providing a *quantitative estimate of his degree of psychiatric disturbance*.

On the other hand, from the standpoint of psychiatric case identification the problems are very different, since we are in essence using a model which is the reverse of that proposed above. Even though there may be infinite gradations between psychiatric illness and normality, in most community surveys the investigator has to use a binomial classification, and to divide the population into 'cases' and 'normals'. It is notable that even those surveys that have begun with a quantitative model end by choosing some threshold point on their continuum that separates cases from normals, and so even these surveys can be reduced to a binomial model. From this point of view, therefore, to the extent that the questionnaire score gives an assessment of a respondent's position on the proposed axis from normality to severe disturbance, it is giving a *probability estimate of the individual being a psychiatric case.*

There are problems associated with both these ways of conceptualizing a score on the questionnaire. The first involves the definition of the 'severity' of psychiatric illness, while the second requires statistical analyses of the validity data that were not presented in the previous chapter. These two problems will therefore be considered at greater length.

The Severity of Psychiatric Illness

There are good reasons for supposing that minor psychiatric symptoms are widely distributed in the population. For example, the *Survey of Sickness 1943–1952* (Logan and Brooke, 1957) showed that only 23 per cent of symptoms that were experienced in the course of a month were taken to a doctor; moreover, in a general practice survey Horder and Horder (1954) showed that in a 3-month period in which there had been 190 consultations for new items of illness, 514 items had not been taken to any medical agency.

One way of dealing with this is to make a rating of severity of illness that is compounded of both intensity of symptoms and the degree of functional impairment caused by these symptoms. This was the approach adopted both in Rennie's Midtown Manhattan Survey and in Leighton's Stirling County Survey. However, as Gruenberg (1963) has pointed out, in practice, intensity and functional impairment are treated by the investigators not as independent variables but as highly correlated variables. In the former study, for example, there are four degrees of 'symptoms' and four degrees of 'interference with life adjustment'. This should have produced 16 possible combinations, but in fact the investigators only consider six combinations, as shown in TABLE 31.

In the standardized psychiatric interview described in the previous chapter it was thought important to define severity in terms of psychiatric phenomenology, without reference to the degree of any associated functional impairment. This has an additional advantage in that, since the issue is not being prejudged, the relationships between psychiatric severity and various sorts of social and behavioural impairments can be investigated by using separate measures of each. (A pilot study of this type, using the clinical interview described here as an index of severity, is described by Sylph, Kedward, and Eastwood (1969).)

The index of severity of illness generated by the standardized psychiatric interview is complicated enough even if functional impairment is neglected, since it is compounded of three separate dimensions. In the first place, it is an 'area' measure, in that the more symptoms that a patient has the higher his score will become. Secondly, for any given symptom higher scores are assigned for degrees of intensity, using degree of associated distress to assess intensity where this is appropriate. Thirdly, for any given symptom higher scores are assigned with increasing degrees of frequency of the symptom in the previous week.

TABLE 31

THE OVERALL SIX-POINT SCALE USED IN THE MIDTOWN
MANHATTAN STUDY

		SYMPTOMS			
---	---	NONE	MILD	MODERATE	SERIOUS
	NONE	0	1	2	
INTERFERENCE:	SOME			3	4
	GREAT				5
	INCAPACITY				6

'Severity' is therefore defined entirely in terms of the phenomena of psychiatric illness, and the assessment of whether a particular patient in a community survey should be considered a 'case' or a 'normal' is made by an experienced psychiatrist in a realistic clinical setting.

An approach which seems more heuristically useful than regarding severity as compounded of intensity of symptoms and degree of functional impairment, is that which distinguishes symptoms on the one hand, and what the patient does with his symptoms—'illness behaviour'—on the other. Mechanic (1962, 1968) writes:

It is plain that symptoms are differently perceived, evaluated and acted upon (or not acted upon) by different kinds of people and in different social situations. Whether because of earlier experiences with illness, because of differential training in respect of symptoms, or because of different biological sensitivities, some persons make light of symptoms, shrug them off, and avoid seeking medical care. Others will respond to little pain and discomfort by readily seeking care, by releasing themselves from work and other obligations, and by becoming dependent on others.

It was pointed out in CHAPTER I that in practice the patient or those in his environment do the 'case identifying' in the community: the psychiatrist merely fixes a diagnostic label on the cases the community offers him, and bases his ideas of severity on these patients. Community surveys usually reveal patients with similar degrees of 'severity' but who have not come under medical care; their 'illness behaviour' has been different.

Among the factors that determine whether a given set of symptoms is taken to a doctor are nationality (Saunders, 1954), social class (Koos, 1954; Kedward,

1962), religion (Mechanic, 1963), and loneliness and nervousness (Mechanic and Volkart, 1961). Even when help has been sought, Lawson (1966) has shown admission to mental hospital to depend not only on nosocomial factors but also on variables such as age of the patient and the time lag between asking for help and the help actually arriving. She concludes that 'non-medical factors—social determinants—play an extensive, often a governing role in the admission of patients as "psychiatric emergencies"'.

In the light of these findings it seems doubly important to keep one's measures of clinical disturbance uncontaminated by social variables like 'functional impairment', and the compound definition of severity of illness proposed above—in terms of number, intensity, and frequency of symptoms —seems to be the most reasonable course to adopt.

If this is accepted, then it must also be conceded that the questionnaire gives a score that correlates highly with a severity rating that was computed on these principles—the product-moment correlation of $+0.80$ quoted in the previous chapter is in effect the basis for claiming that the questionnaire gives a quantitative assessment of the severity of psychiatric disturbance.

The situation, therefore, is that the questionnaire score has been correlated against a criterion which has itself been shown to be reliable and to consist of the traditional phenomena of psychiatric illness carefully separated from social variables, such as degree of impairment, and from factors referring to the patient's social relationships.

It is interesting, therefore, to examine the content of the items in the questionnaire which produce the score that correlated so well with these phenomena.

It will be recalled that in the search for items described in CHAPTER III the net was cast widely, and in addition to the traditional phenomena of illness questions were asked about observable behaviour, ability to cope with problems, and 'role-satisfaction'. Most of the alternative scales have not done this, but have tended to confine themselves to the usual clinical ideas about the nature of mental illness.

The calibration study reported in CHAPTER III in effect provided information about those features that discriminated best between people who are looked upon as mentally ill and those who are not.

The original 140 questions included such traditional symptoms of mental illness as:

HAVE YOU RECENTLY:

- found yourself waking early, and unable to go back to sleep?
- felt as though you were not really there, or as though things around you weren't real?
- had the feeling that people were looking at you?
- been worrying unduly about things that don't really matter?
- been afraid that something awful is going to happen?

— had difficulty in stopping your hands from shaking and trembling?
— found that unwelcome thoughts keep coming into your mind?
— found that the idea of taking your own life kept coming into your mind?

Yet none of these items found their way into the best 30 discriminators between the calibration groups [see APPENDIX 6].

The questions that emerge as the most telling way of discriminating psychiatrically disturbed patients from 'normal' patients reveal questions such as the following among the 'best 12' [see APPENDIX 6]:

HAVE YOU RECENTLY:

— felt that you couldn't overcome your difficulties?
— felt that you are playing a useful part in things?
— been losing confidence in yourself?
— been able to enjoy your day-to-day activities?
— been able to face up to your problems?
— felt constantly under strain?

Admittedly, this is a selected list, and conventional items like feelings of depression and worthlessness also occur in the best 12 items—but the contrast between the two lists given above is still striking.

The conclusion seems inescapable. Although there may be strong theoretical reasons for measuring severity of illness in terms of the traditional phenomena of illness, many of the items that best define illness are inextricably connected with the patient's perceiving himself to be unable to cope with his problems and to deal with social difficulties.

The Probability of being a Psychiatric Case

To say that patients in a general practitioner's surgery with scores of 11 and below are 'probable normals', and that those with scores of 12 and above are 'probable cases', is obviously an absurd oversimplification. There can be nothing magical about the possession of 11 symptoms, so that the twelfth is invariably the straw that breaks the camel's back. All that it can mean is that between 11 and 12 symptoms the probability of being a case is 0·5, and that above this it will be greater than 0·5, and below this it will be below 0·5.

With a sufficiently large population, it would be possible to consider each possible score on the questionnaire separately, and work out the probability of a respondent with that score being a case. Unfortunately the total population in the two validation studies was only 291, so it is impractical to work out probabilities for each score separately, since the numbers in each group would be insufficiently large. It was possible to work out a family of probabilities by taking the scores in groups of six, so that 0–5, 6–11, 12–17, and so on, were grouped together in all groups except those scoring more than 30, who all had to be lumped together. When this was done the numbers in each group were large enough, and it was possible to work out 95 per cent confidence limits for each probability. The effect of doing this is to say that a respondent with a particular score has a 95 per cent chance of falling within the range of probabilities indicated by the confidence limits. The resultant graph is shown in FIGURE 9.

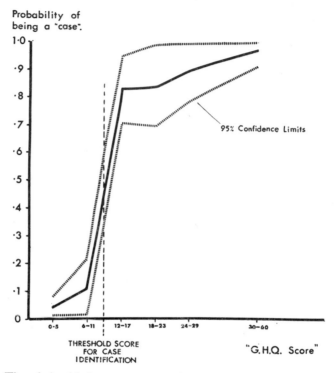

FIG. 9. The relationship between score on the questionnaire and the probability of being assessed as a psychiatric case (the 95 per cent confidence limits are shown).

Between the score group 6–11 and the group 12–17 the probability of being a case rises very steeply indeed from 0·11 up to 0·83. It must be remembered that, seductive as this graph is, it is based on a population with a high prevalence of disease. It is easy to see intuitively that the probability of an individual with a GHQ score of, say, 15 being a case is higher in a population with a high prevalence of disease than in one with a low prevalence. Given the specificity of the scale, he is more likely to be a 'false positive' in the latter than in the former situation.

The 'Hits Positive' Rate

Meehl and Rosen (1955) have applied Bayes' Theorem to the problem of screening populations for disease. This theorem, when applied to a situation where a population is to be divided into two categories, states that:

$$Pd_{(i)} = \frac{P_{p_1}}{P_{p_1} + Q_{p_2}},$$

where

$Pd_{(i)}$ = probability that a given individual is diseased, given that his screening score is positive ('hits positive' rate).

P = proportion of actual cases in the population being examined (prevalence).

p_1 = proportion of actual cases with high scores (sensitivity of the test).

p_2 = proportion of normals misidentified by the test as cases (false positive rate).

And let

$Q = 1 - P$ (proportion of non-cases in population).

$q_1 = 1 - p_1$ (false negative rate).

$q_2 = 1 - p_2$ (specificity of the test).

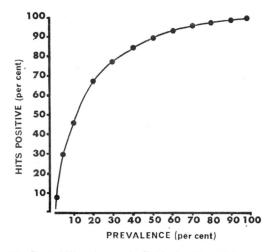

FIG. 10. Probability that an individual with a high score will turn out to be a case ('hits positive rate') by prevalence for the questionnaire, assuming 95·7 per cent sensitivity and 88·2 per cent specificity.

For example, if the prevalence of disorder in a given population is 34 per cent, the probability that a given individual in that population with a high score on the questionnaire will be found to be a case will be:

$$\frac{0·34 \times 0·957}{0·34 \times 0·957 + 0·66 \times 0·122} = 0·80.$$

Another way of expressing this is that, for a population with a prevalence of 34 per cent, 80 per cent of those with high scores will be found to be cases. The proportion of those with high scores that turn out to be cases is sometimes called the 'hits positive' rate of the test, and it rises sharply with increasing prevalence, as shown in FIGURE 10. It can be seen from this figure that for the present questionnaire below prevalences of 12 per cent there will be a less than even chance that a high scorer will actually be a case. The relationship between the predictive value of a screening test in medicine and prevalence has also been discussed by Vecchio (1966) and Whitby (1968).

Overall Misclassification

In the special case of a screening test with its sensitivity equal to its specificity, alterations in the prevalence of disease in the population would make no difference to the proportion of cases misclassified by the test. However, with a prevalence of zero the misclassifications will be entirely determined by the specificity of the test, and at a prevalence of 100 per cent they

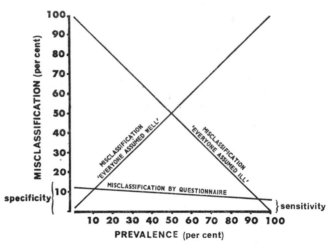

FIG. 11. The relationship between percentage of cases misclassified by questionnaire and prevalence, assuming 95·7 per cent sensitivity and 88·2 per cent specificity.

will be determined by the sensitivity. At intermediate prevalences each will play a part, so that, using the same notation as that used above:

$$\text{overall misclassification rate} = Qp_2 + Pq_1.$$

Using the specificity and sensitivity figures obtained for the questionnaire in Dr. Blackwell's practice, the variation of misclassification rate with prevalence is shown in FIGURE 11. This figure also shows the probability of correct classification if no screening test is used, but all patients are arbitrarily assumed to be either 'well' or 'ill'. It can be seen that the screening test has its greatest value in the middle ranges, but that at each end of the scale use of the questionnaire actually increases the number of misclassifications.

It is possible to derive formulae from Bayes' Theorem to show that unless

$$P < \frac{q_2}{q_1 + q_2} \quad \text{and} \quad Q < \frac{p_1}{p_1 + p_2},$$

the making of decisions on the basis of a screening test will have an adverse effect. Fortunately for the present questionnaire, the clinical and community populations on which the test has been used to date have had prevalences of between 20 per cent and 45 per cent, and between these limits the screening test works quite well.

Alterations of the Threshold Score. The threshold scores quoted so far—11/12 for the 60-item questionnaire, and 3/4 for the 30-item questionnaire—provide optimum discrimination for most screening purposes, but there are circumstances in which it would be reasonable to alter these thresholds.

If a prevalence survey were aimed at missing as few cases as possible, one would naturally lower the threshold so as to increase the sensitivity of the test at the expense of the specificity. How much one did this would depend on how low a 'hits positive' rate the investigator could tolerate from the standpoint of economic feasibility.

If, on the other hand, a particular investigation required a screening test that would yield a homogeneously ill population, then this could be achieved to some extent by raising the threshold score. For example, at a prevalence of 34 per cent, raising the threshold score from 12 to 20 increases the 'hits positive' rate from 80 per cent to 85 per cent, but it does this at the expense of increasing the overall misclassification rate to 15·5 per cent.

Problems of Screening Populations with a Low Prevalence of Disease

At extremes of prevalence the screening test may actually make prediction worse [FIG. 11]. There is a paradox here, as if the screening test is part of a two-stage procedure it may nevertheless result in cases being detected that would otherwise have been missed. The advantages of detecting these cases must therefore be weighed against the costs of the procedure, which may be broken down into:

1. The cost of administering the questionnaire.
2. The cost of administering the second stage procedure for case identification.
3. The inconvenience to the respondent of declaring healthy people potentially ill.

We have already seen that at low prevalences the 'hits positive' rate drops considerably, thus considerably increasing the costs and inconvenience mentioned above. Although overall misclassification rate at low prevalences can be decreased by raising the threshold score—and therefore improving the specificity [see FIG. 11]—in practice no one would consider doing this because the lowered sensitivity might lose the few cases that there were to find.

Predicting Prevalence from the Proportion of High Scores

If the sensitivity and specificity of the questionnaire are known for a particular population, it will often be required to predict the prevalence of disorder on the basis of the proportion of the population who are found to have high scores. It is easy to see that at zero prevalence the number of respondents with high scores will be determined by the specificity, while at 100 per cent prevalence the number with high scores will be determined by the sensitivity. Thus, when the prevalence is low the percentage with high scores will be greater than the prevalence, whereas when it is high the percentage will be less. This relationship is shown for the present questionnaire in FIGURE 12.

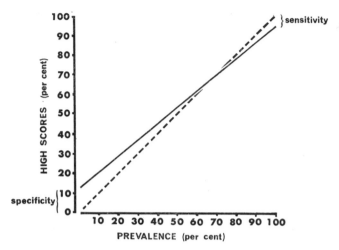

FIG. 12. The relationship between percentage of a population with high scores and prevalence for the 60-item questionnaire in general practice.

Using the same notation as before, the relationship between the two variables is:

$$\text{proportion with high scores} = Qp_2 + Pp_1.$$

It must be emphasized that the sensitivity and specificity values quoted for the questionnaire in TABLES 27 and 28 should not be generalized to different types of consulting populations. For example, because a sensitivity of 95 per cent was found in a London general practice this does not mean that a similar sensitivity would be found among psychiatric out-patients: here one would expect a lower sensitivity because of larger numbers of defensive patients and of those with chronic psychiatric illnesses.

The Effects of Major Demographic Variables on Questionnaire Score

The effects of major demographic variables on the mean GHQ scores of patients attending general practitioners is shown in APPENDIX 7. The means were very much lower in Philadelphia than in London because the questionnaire used in the United States was a shorter version with only 30 items.

In both locations women had a higher score than men, the difference being significant at the 0·01 level. Divorced and separated patients had higher mean scores than either married or single patients, yet the mean score for widows and widowers was the same as that for married patients.

When one considers the effects of variables such as age and social class, it seems reasonable to carry out tests to see whether there are effects on the mean score that operate over the whole range of ages or social classes. Tests using an analysis of variance have shown that age has no effect on mean score in either location. In Philadelphia social class as measured by Hollingshead and Redlich's social index had a significant effect on the mean score, with a tendency for the means to be higher among the lower social classes. Although the mean score for blacks was slightly higher than that for whites over the whole data, this had to be interpreted with caution since the two groups were not matched for social class. However, an analysis of co-variance showed that this difference between the races remained ($F = 5 \cdot 67$ on 1; 905 df; $P < 0 \cdot 05$) when an allowance was made for the effects of differences in the social class make-up of the two samples. It is difficult to draw any conclusion concerning the effects of social class on the London data, since there was an over-representation of Social Class II and an under-representation of Social Classes I and V among the patients attending Dr. Blackwell, who were selected for the psychiatric interview. It can be seen from APPENDIX 7 that, among those patients who were seen, there was no tendency for low social class to be associated with an increased score.

A COMPARISON OF THE GENERAL HEALTH QUESTION-NAIRE WITH OTHER SCALES AND INVENTORIES

Direct comparisons of the present questionnaire with the various alternatives described in CHAPTER II are not really possible, since the experimental methods used to provide the data on reliability and validity of the various scales differ so widely. Very few of the scales described have undergone validity studies in which a series of patients, containing both normal individuals and people with various degrees of psychiatric disturbance, was given both the scale in question and an independent psychiatric assessment. Apart from the present questionnaire, the only scales to be so tested are Rawnsley's modification of the CMI and Macmillan's HOS. Rawnsley's results are probably the most closely comparable with those for the GHQ, but in interpreting Macmillan's it is difficult to know what to do with the 23 patients classified by him at interview as 'doubtful'. In the data presented in TABLE 32, the range given for Macmillan's work with the HOS is calculated by considering his data both with and without the doubtful cases. Where possible, the various scales have been considered in terms of 'sensitivity' and 'specificity', since these parameters are independent of the prevalence of the disease in the population concerned. The overall misclassification rate has been computed for a prevalence of 25 per cent for each questionnaire to facilitate comparisons between questionnaires. It was obtained by using the formula

overall misclassification $_{(25\%)}$
$$= 0 \cdot 75 \, (100 - \text{specificity}) + 0 \cdot 25 \, (100 - \text{sensitivity}).$$

TABLE 32

A COMPARISON OF THE GENERAL HEALTH QUESTIONNAIRE WITH OTHER
SCALES FROM THE POINT OF VIEW OF CASE IDENTIFICATION

SCREENING TEST	COR-RELATION WITH CLINICAL STATUS	SENSI-TIVITY %	SPECI-FICITY %	OVERALL MIS-CLASSIFICATION (assuming 25 per cent prevalence) %
60-item GHQ General practice (London) 200 pts.	+0·80	95·7	87·8	10·3
60-item GHQ Medical OPD (London) 91 pts.	+0·77	87·1	93·3	8·2
30-item GHQ 5 general practices (Philadelphia) 247 pts.	+0·77	85·0	79·5	19·1
36-item SCL 5 general practices (Philadelphia) 247 pts.	—	84·0	68·8	28·0
Kellner's SRT (83 pts.)	—	95·0	76·7	18·7
Saslow's Screening Test (447 pts.)	—	72·0	95·0	11·0
Shepherd Cornell Medical Inventory	+0·19[2]	70·0	—	—
Rawnsley's Modified CMI (76 pts.)[1]	—	73·5	81·7	17·8
Macmillan's HOS (64 pts.)[1]	+0·50	75–84	54–68	22–40
Langner's 22-item screen test (1660 pts.)[1]	—	73·5	81·7	17·8
Foulds's SSI (336 pts.)[1]	—	89·0	86·0	13·2
Beck's Depression Inventory (409 pts.)[1]	+0·66[2]	—	—	at least 23·0

[1] An administered scale.   [2] Biserial correlation.

TABLE 32 shows that the results obtained with Kellner's SRT and with Foulds's SSI are only a little less good than those obtained with the present questionnaire. These figures must be interpreted with caution, however, for they are both obtained by examining the scores of a group of 'normals' and a group of identified 'cases', so that it is reasonable to suppose that patients with intermediate degrees of disturbance are not represented in their data. By way of contrast, if the patients rated as 'subclinically disturbed' at the standard psychiatric interview in the general practice validity survey with the GHQ are excluded from consideration, the overall misclassification rate drops to 4·9 per cent. It is not the present contention that this figure can be compared with those given for the SRT or the SSI; it is merely given to demonstrate that the exclusion of patients with intermediate degrees of disturbance makes a great difference to the data obtained concerning case identification, since these are the very patients about whom difficulties may arise.

THE LIMITATIONS AND USES OF THE PRESENT QUESTIONNAIRE

Limitations

The psychiatric patients that the questionnaire tends to miss can be divided into three groups. The first group consists of defensive people who are not prepared to describe their symptoms in a pencil and paper test situation. These patients tend to behave in a 'defensive' way in a face-to-face situation as well as on the questionnaire. It would appear that this problem is an inherent limitation of the questionnaire method: fortunately they were a very small group compared with other classes of respondents.

The second group consists of patients with dementia, chronic schizophrenia, and hypomania. The questionnaire is not designed to detect these patients, and there is reason to believe that it does not do so.

The third group of patients consists of those with very longstanding disorders, especially if the patient perceives himself as going through a good phase of his illness. This is undoubtedly due to the fact that with the GHQ method of scoring the questionnaire the patient does not score unless his symptoms are 'rather more' or 'much more than usual'. This effect is reflected in the fact that the less acute the patients' disturbances are in a particular setting, the lower is the threshold score that best discriminates between cases and normals. Thus, in a general practice setting, a medical out-patients' department, and a psychiatric supportive out-patients' department, optimal discrimination was obtained with progressively lower threshold scores. It might be thought that the existence of this third group of patients would represent a formidable limitation of the questionnaire, but the curious fact is that only a small minority of patients with chronic disorders are misclassified because they have responded 'same as usual'. Most of them seem to sustain a notion of their 'usual selves' as people who are free from symptoms, even after illnesses that have lasted many years. The patients who are misclassified ('false negatives') usually had a combination of a longstanding complaint and defensiveness at interview.

Uses

As a result of the experience gained in the validity studies it is possible to describe the clinical features of the psychiatric illnesses that were detected in the group of respondents found to have high scores (see APPENDIX 5: clinical vignettes, for examples). Undoubtedly the largest group could be described as affective neuroses—that is to say, minor depressions, anxiety states, and patients who would at one time have been diagnosed as 'neurasthenics'. A useful feature of the questionnaire is that it detects patients whose otherwise inexplicable somatic symptoms are accompanied by an affective disturbance that they have not presented to the physician. These patients have been described as having 'hidden psychiatric illnesses' (Goldberg and Blackwell, 1970), and it has been shown that treatment of the patient's psychiatric illness often improves his physical condition as well. It is, of course, well known that acute psychotic episodes and organic psychoses can present with an initial affective disturbance, and it has been found that when this occurs these patients are also detected by the questionnaire.

A patient's score on the General Health Questionnaire is in many ways analogous to the erythrocyte sedimentation rate (ESR) in general medicine. In both cases, the high score merely indicates that there is a high probability that there is something wrong with the patient, but it does not tell the physician the diagnosis. It is an instruction to the physician to examine the patient, and make a diagnosis, using his clinical skills. Just as it is possible for a patient with serious physical disease to have a normal ESR, so there is a small group of patients with psychiatric illnesses who may have scores in the normal range. Fortunately, the probability that a patient with a normal score will turn out to be a psychiatric case is fairly low. A final point of similarity with the ESR is that if the GHQ score is high in a given patient, then serial test administration provides a good index of the progress of the patient's illness.

The questionnaire would appear to be useful to two distinct groups of doctors. It could assist general practitioners and physicians in the identification of patients with minor psychiatric illnesses, and for epidemiologists and social psychiatrists it could have applications in research. It would not appear to have many uses in populations of identified psychiatric cases, since it was never intended to supplant the clinical interview; other rating techniques will usually be more appropriate with such patients. The questionnaire has four distinct research uses. First, it can be used to compare the amount of non-psychotic psychiatric disturbance in two populations by comparing the means and standard deviations of scores in each population. Secondly, psychiatric disturbance as assessed by score on the questionnaire can be correlated with other clinical and social variables in a given population. Thirdly, a given population can be tested on different occasions in order to follow the changes that occur in psychiatric disturbance with time. Finally, the questionnaire can be used to assess the *point prevalence* of minor psychiatric illness in cross-sectional studies, and should in this case ideally be the first part of a two-stage process of case identification. By itself it is of no value in making assessments of the lifetime prevalence of psychiatric illness.

THE LONG FORM (140 ITEMS) OF THE GENERAL HEALTH QUESTIONNAIRE
WITH INTRODUCTORY PARAGRAPHS FOR
'THE SEVERELY ILL'

GENERAL HEALTH QUESTIONNAIRE

We should like to know if you have had any medical complaints, and how your health has been in general, *over the past few weeks*. Please answer *all* questions below simply by underlining the answer which you think most nearly applies to you. Remember we want to know about present or recent complaints not those you had in the past.

Name: Age:

Occupation:

(For married women) Husband's occupation:

Today's date:

GENERAL HEALTH QUESTIONNAIRE

HAVE YOU RECENTLY:

A.

1. — *been feeling perfectly well and in good health?*	Better than usual	Same as usual	Worse than usual	Much worse than usual
2. — *been feeling in need of a good tonic?*	Not at all	No more than usual	Rather more than usual	Much more than usual
3. — *been feeling run-down and out of sorts?*	Not at all	No more than usual	Rather more than usual	Much more than usual
4. — *felt that you are ill?*	Not at all	No more than usual	Rather more than usual	Much more than usual
5. — *been worried about losing weight?*	Not at all	No more than usual	Rather more than usual	Much more than usual
6. — *been putting on too much weight?*	Not at all	No more than usual	Rather more than usual	Much more than usual

HAVE YOU RECENTLY:

7. — *been getting any pains in your head?*	Not at all	No more than usual	Rather more than usual	Much more than usual
8. — *been getting any really bad headaches?*	Not at all	No more than usual	Rather more than usual	Much more than usual
9. — *been getting any noises in your ears?*	Not at all	No more than usual	Rather more than usual	Much more than usual
10. — *been getting a feeling of tight-ness or pressure in your head?*	Not at all	No more than usual	Rather more than usual	Much more than usual
11. — *found you couldn't give your mind to anything?*	Not at all	No more than usual	Rather more than usual	Much more than usual
12. — *noticed pins and needles in your hands and feet?*	Not at all	No more than usual	Rather more than usual	Much more than usual
13. — *had difficulty in stopping your hands from shaking or trembling?*	Not at all	No more than usual	Rather more than usual	Much more than usual
14. — *found that you have been bothered by noise?*	Not at all	No more than usual	Rather more than usual	Much more than usual
15. — *found yourself blushing easily?*	Not at all	No more than usual	Rather more than usual	Much more than usual
16. — *thought that you might have some terrible disease?*	Not at all	No more than usual	Rather more than usual	Much more than usual
17. — *been able to concentrate on whatever you're doing?*	Better than usual	Same as usual	Less than usual	Much less than usual

B.

1. — *been feeling worried about your heart?*	Not at all	No more than usual	Rather more than usual	Much more than usual
2. — *been afraid that you were going to collapse in a public place?*	Not at all	No more than usual	Rather more than usual	Much more than usual
3. — *been aware of your heart thumping?*	Not at all	No more than usual	Rather more than usual	Much more than usual

HAVE YOU RECENTLY:

4. — *had any palpitations?*	Not at all	No more than usual	Rather more than usual	Much more than usual
5. — *felt frightened that your heart might suddenly stop?*	Not at all	No more than usual	Rather more than usual	Much more than usual
6. — *been having hot or cold spells?*	Not at all	No more than usual	Rather more than usual	Much more than usual
7. — *been perspiring (sweating) a lot?*	Not at all	No more than usual	Rather more than usual	Much more than usual
8. — *been getting short of breath?*	Not at all	No more than usual	Rather more than usual	Much more than usual
9. — *been suffering from backache?*	Not at all	No more than usual	Rather more than usual	Much more than usual
10. — *been suffering from aches and pains in any part of your body?*	Not at all	No more than usual	Rather more than usual	Much more than usual
11. — *been off your food?*	Not at all	No more than usual	Rather more than usual	Much more than usual
12. — *been feeling nauseated (sick)?*	Not at all	No more than usual	Rather more than usual	Much more than usual
13. — *been getting indigestion?*	Not at all	No more than usual	Rather more than usual	Much more than usual
14. — *felt as though your food is doing you no good?*	Not at all	No more than usual	Rather more than usual	Much more than usual
15. — *had any griping pains in your abdomen (belly)?*	Not at all	No more than usual	Rather more than usual	Much more than usual
16. — *been troubled a lot by wind?*	Not at all	No more than usual	Rather more than usual	Much more than usual
17. — *had any diarrhoea (loose motions)?*	Not at all	No more than usual	Rather more than usual	Much more than usual
18. — *suffered from constipation?*	Not at all	No more than usual	Rather more than usual	Much more than usual

C.

1. — *found yourself waking early and unable to get back to sleep?*	Not at all	No more than usual	Rather more than usual	Much more than usual
2. — *been getting up feeling your sleep hasn't refreshed you?*	Not at all	No more than usual	Rather more than usual	Much more than usual
3. — *been taking a long time to get going in the mornings?*	Not at all	No more than usual	Rather more than usual	Much more than usual

HAVE YOU RECENTLY:

4. — *been feeling too tired and exhausted even to eat?*	Not at all	No more than usual	Rather more than usual	Much more than usual
5. — *found yourself lacking in energy?*	Not at all	No more than usual	Rather more than usual	Much more than usual
6. — *lost much sleep over worry?*	Not at all	No more than usual	Rather more than usual	Much more than usual
7. — *been feeling mentally alert and wide awake?*	Better than usual	Same as usual	Less alert than usual	Much less alert
8. — *been feeling full of energy?*	Better than usual	Same as usual	Less energy than usual	Much less energetic
9. — *been feeling restless and unable to relax?*	Not at all	No more than usual	Rather more than usual	Much more than usual
10. — *been feeling easily fatigued (tired out)?*	Not at all	No more than usual	Rather more than usual	Much more than usual
11. — *been having spells of complete exhaustion?*	Not at all	No more than usual	Rather more than usual	Much more than usual
12. — *been feeling too tired out in the evenings to do anything but sit?*	Not at all	No more than usual	Rather more than usual	Much more than usual
13. — *been feeling tired and ready for bed earlier than usual?*	Not at all	No more than usual	Rather more than usual	Much more than usual
14. — *had difficulty in getting off to sleep?*	Not at all	No more than usual	Rather more than usual	Much more than usual
15. — *been having to take sleeping pills to get a night's rest?*	Not at all	No more than usual	Rather more than usual	Much more than usual
16. — *had difficulty in staying asleep once you are off?*	Not at all	No more than usual	Rather more than usual	Much more than usual
17. — *been having frightening or unpleasant dreams?*	Not at all	No more than usual	Rather more than usual	Much more than usual
18. — *been getting up at night to pass water?*	Not at all	No more than usual	Rather more than usual	Much more than usual
19. — *been having restless, disturbed nights?*	Not at all	No more than usual	Rather more than usual	Much more than usual

HAVE YOU RECENTLY:

D.

1. — *been giving vent to your feelings by banging things about or slamming doors?*	Not at all	No more than usual	Rather more than usual	Much more than usual
2. — *been feeling at times on the brink of tears?*	Not at all	No more than usual	Rather more than usual	Much more than usual
3. — *given way to tears when you've been on your own?*	Not at all	No more than usual	Rather more than usual	Much more than usual
4. — *been managing to keep yourself busy and occupied?*	More so than usual	Same as usual	Rather less than usual	Much less than usual
5. — *found yourself having to do some things repeatedly before you're satisfied?*	Less than usual	About same as usual	Rather more than usual	Much more than usual
6. — *found yourself putting things off as long as possible?*	Not at all	No more than usual	Rather more than usual	Much more than usual
7. — *been taking longer over the things you do?*	Quicker than usual	About same as usual	Longer than usual	Much longer than usual
8. — *tended to lose interest in your ordinary activities?*	Not at all	No more than usual	Rather more than usual	Much more than usual
9. — *tended to sit about and do nothing?*	Not at all	No more than usual	Rather more than usual	Much more than usual
10. — *been losing interest in your personal appearance?*	Not at all	No more than usual	Rather more than usual	Much more than usual
11. — *been taking less trouble with your clothes?*	More trouble than usual	About same as usual	Less trouble than usual	Much less trouble
12. — *been biting your nails or picking at your fingers?*	Not at all	No more than usual	Rather more than usual	Much more than usual
13. — *been getting out of the house as much as usual?*	More than usual	Same as usual	Less than usual	Much less than usual
14. — *been going out in the evenings to enjoy yourself?*	More than usual	Same as usual	Less than usual	Much less than usual

HAVE YOU RECENTLY:

15. — *been able to go into shops on your own?*	More than usual	Same as usual	Less than usual	Much less than usual
16. — *felt afraid to go out alone?*	Not at all	No more than usual	Rather more than usual	Much more than usual
17. — *been managing as well as most people would in your shoes?*	Better than most	About the same	Rather less well	Much less well
18. — *felt on the whole you were doing things well?*	Better than usual	About the same	Less well than usual	Much less well
19. — *had to take time off work, or leave your housework undone?*	None at all	No more than usual	Rather more than usual	Much more than usual
20. — *been late getting to work, or getting started on your housework?*	Not at all	No later than usual	Rather later than usual	Much later than usual
21. — *found difficulty in keeping up with your work?*	Less difficult than usual	About same as usual	More difficult than usual	Much more difficulty
22. — *been satisfied with the way you've carried out your task?*	More satisfied than usual	About same as usual	Less satisfied than usual	Much less satisfied

E.

1. — *been worried about the effect you are having on those close to you?*	Not at all	No more than usual	Rather more than usual	Much more than usual
2. — *been getting on well with those close to you?*	Better than usual	About same as usual	Less well than usual	Much less well
3. — *been able to feel warmth and affection for those near to you?*	Better than usual	About same as usual	Less well than usual	Much less well
4. — *been worrying about what is going to happen to your family, or people you care about most?*	Not at all	No more than usual	Rather more than usual	Much more than usual
5. — *been losing your temper or getting into arguments?*	Not at all	No more than usual	Rather more than usual	Much more than usual

HAVE YOU RECENTLY:

6. — *been feeling that you are a burden on others?*	Not at all	No more than usual	Rather more than usual	Much more than usual
7. — *had to be on your guard even with your friends?*	Not at all	No more than usual	Rather more than usual	Much more than usual
8. — *been getting on well with friends and acquaintances?*	Better than usual	About same as usual	Less well than usual	Much less well
9. — *been getting on all right with your neighbours?*	Better than usual	About same as usual	Less well than usual	Much less well
10. — *been finding it easy to get on with other people?*	Better than usual	About same as usual	Less well than usual	Much less well
11. — *spent much time chatting with people?*	More time than usual	About same as usual	Less than usual	Much less than usual
12. — *found other people tend to regard you as a touchy person?*	Definitely not	Probably not	Possibly	Probably
13. — *felt a need to talk to other people about your own troubles?*	Less than usual	No more than usual	Rather more than usual	Much more than usual
14. — *kept feeling afraid to say anything to people in case you made a fool of yourself?*	Not at all	No more than usual	Rather more than usual	Much more than usual
15. — *found that other people seemed to have misunderstood you?*	Not at all	No more than usual	Rather more than usual	Much more than usual
16. — *been brooding over things that people have said to you?*	Not at all	No more than usual	Rather more than usual	Much more than usual
17. — *noticed that other people seem to be getting on your nerves?*	Not at all	No more than usual	Rather more than usual	Much more than usual
18. — *had difficulty about speaking to strangers?*	Not at all	No more than usual	Rather more than usual	Much more than usual
19. — *felt that you are properly appreciated and valued by others?*	More than usual	About same as usual	Rather less than usual	Much less than usual

HAVE YOU RECENTLY:

20. — *been feeling that you were no good to anybody?*	Not at all	No more than usual	Rather more than usual	Much more than usual

F.

1. — *felt that you are playing a useful part in things?*	More so than usual	Same as usual	Less useful than usual	Much less useful
2. — *felt contented with your lot?*	More so than usual	Same as usual	Less so than usual	Much less contented
3. — *felt capable of making decisions about things?*	More so than usual	Same as usual	Less so than usual	Much less capable
4. — *felt you're just not able to make a start on anything?*	Not at all	No more than usual	Rather more than usual	Much more than usual
5. — *felt yourself dreading every-thing that you have to do?*	Not at all	No more than usual	Rather more than usual	Much more than usual
6. — *felt constantly under strain?*	Not at all	No more than usual	Rather more than usual	Much more than usual
7. — *felt you couldn't overcome your difficulties?*	Not at all	No more than usual	Rather more than usual	Much more than usual
8. — *felt afraid of expressing your-self in case you made a foolish mistake?*	Not at all	No more than usual	Rather more than usual	Much more than usual
9. — *felt frightened to be on your own?*	Not at all	No more than usual	Rather more than usual	Much more than usual
10. — *felt confident about going into public places?*	More so than usual	Same as usual	Less so than usual	Much less than usual
11. — *felt afraid to read the papers or watch television because of what you might see?*	Not at all	No more than usual	Rather more than usual	Much more than usual
12. — *felt as though you were not really there, or as though things around you weren't real?*	Not at all	No more than usual	Rather more than usual	Much more than usual
13. — *been finding life a struggle all the time?*	Not at all	No more than usual	Rather more than usual	Much more than usual

HAVE YOU RECENTLY:

14. — *been blaming yourself for things that have gone wrong?*	Not at all	No more than usual	Rather more than usual	Much more than usual
15. — *been able to enjoy your normal day-to-day activities?*	More so than usual	Same as usual	Less so than usual	Much less than usual
16. — *been taking things hard?*	Not at all	No more than usual	Rather more than usual	Much more than usual
17. — *been getting edgy and bad tempered?*	Not at all	No more than usual	Rather more than usual	Much more than usual
18. — *been getting scared or panicky for no good reason?*	Not at all	No more than usual	Rather more than usual	Much more than usual
19. — *been able to face up to your problems?*	More so than usual	Same as usual	Less able than usual	Much less able
20. — *been having a lot of worry about money?*	Not at all	No more than usual	Rather more than usual	Much more than usual
21. — *found everything getting on top of you?*	Not at all	No more than usual	Rather more than usual	Much more than usual
22. — *found yourself getting easily upset about things?*	Not at all	No more than usual	Rather more than usual	Much more than usual
23. — *found little annoyances making you upset or angry?*	Not at all	No more than usual	Rather more than usual	Much more than usual
24. — *had the feeling that people were looking at you?*	Not at all	No more than usual	Rather more than usual	Much more than usual
25. — *noticed that your feelings are easily hurt?*	Not at all	No more than usual	Rather more than usual	Much more than usual

G.

1. — *been feeling unhappy and depressed?*	Not at all	No more than usual	Rather more than usual	Much more than usual
2. — *been losing confidence in yourself?*	Not at all	No more than usual	Rather more than usual	Much more than usual
3. — *been thinking of yourself as a worthless person?*	Not at all	No more than usual	Rather more than usual	Much more than usual

HAVE YOU RECENTLY:

4. — *felt that life is entirely hopeless?*	Not at all	No more than usual	Rather more than usual	Much more than usual
5. — *been feeling hopeful about your own future?*	More so than usual	About same as usual	Less so than usual	Much less hopeful
6. — *been feeling reasonably happy, all things considered?*	More so than usual	About same as usual	Less so than usual	Much less happy
7. — *been worrying unduly about things that don't really matter?*	Not at all	No more than usual	Rather more than usual	Much more than usual
8. — *been afraid that you might be losing control of yourself?*	Not at all	No more than usual	Rather more than usual	Much more than usual
9. — *been afraid that something awful is going to happen?*	Not at all	No more than usual	Rather more than usual	Much more than usual
10. — *been worrying that you might be going to have a nervous breakdown?*	Not at all	No more than usual	Rather more than usual	Much more than usual
11. — *been feeling nervous and strung up all the time?*	Not at all	No more than usual	Rather more than usual	Much more than usual
12. — *found yourself getting anxious that someone may have been harmed?*	Not at all	No more than usual	Rather more than usual	Much more than usual
13. — *felt that life isn't worth living?*	Not at all	No more than usual	Rather more than usual	Much more than usual
14. — *thought of the possibility that you might make away with yourself?*	Definitely not	I don't think so	Has crossed my mind	Definitely have
15. — *found at times you couldn't do anything because your nerves were too bad?*	Not at all	No more than usual	Rather more than usual	Much more than usual
16. — *found that your thoughts keep going round and round certain things?*	Not at all	No more than usual	Rather more than usual	Much more than usual

HAVE YOU RECENTLY:

17. — *found that unwelcome thoughts keep coming into your mind?*

| Not at all | No more than usual | Rather more than usual | Much more than usual |

18. — *found yourself wishing you were dead and away from it all?*

| Not at all | No more than usual | Rather more than usual | Much more than usual |

19. — *found that the idea of taking your own life kept coming into your mind?*

| Definitely not | I don't think so | Has crossed my mind | Definitely has |

Thank you for your co-operation.
Could you please answer two more questions?

How tiring did you find this questionnaire?

| No bother at all | I got rather tired towards the end but think my answers were accurate | Tired towards the end and may not have been accurate | Very tiring. Many of the items difficult |

Do you think that you are at all ill?

| Healthier and more stable than average | About average | Slightly more nervous or ill than average | Fairly ill: would be helped by medical treatment | Very ill: need to be in hospital |

APPENDIX 2

THE STRUCTURED INTERVIEW USED TO SELECT 'NORMALS'

GENERAL HEALTH QUESTIONNAIRE—SCREENING INTERVIEW

ACTION

1. *Would you say that your general health is good, fair or poor?*

(Indicate response)	GOOD	Carry on
	FAIR	Carry on
	POOR	Reject subject.

2. *When did you last see your doctor for your health?*

A: ....

If more than 3 months ago, carry on to Q. 3, otherwise:

And when before that?

A: ....

If two or more visits for different things in past 3 months, REJECT.

3. *Are you taking any medicines or tablets now?*

A: ....

....

If YES, find if they are taken regularly, and if a doctor prescribed them.

REJECT all on 'nerve tablets', and all on regular persistent medication prescribed by a doctor.

4. *Do you go out to work? Have you lost any time through sickness lately?*

A: ....

....

If NO, carry on to Q. 5.
If YES, REJECT any with a loss of more than 2 weeks in the past 3 months.

5. *Is there anything that your health stops you from doing now?*

A: ....

....

....

Merely record reply.

ACTION

6. *Have you any kind of nerve trouble?*

  — feeling keyed up or anxious?   If YES, REJECT

  — not being able to get off to   If persistent insomnia or regular sleeping
     sleep at night?   tablets, REJECT.

  — or anything like that?

  A: ....   Merely record reply.

     ....

IF THE SUBJECT IS ACCEPTED FOR THE QUESTIONNAIRE, BE SURE TO WRITE THE NUMBER OF THE QUESTIONNAIRE GIVEN TO THEM HERE

Number of Questionnaire ....

Age: *Sex:*

Occupation:

(For married women only)
Husband's occupation:

DEMOGRAPHIC DATA FOR THE THREE CALIBRATION GROUPS

SEX:

	Females	Males
Severely ill	52	48
Mildly ill	49	51
Mean of ill groups	$50\frac{1}{2}$	$49\frac{1}{2}$
Normals	51	49

SOCIAL CLASS:

	1	*2*	*3*	*4*	*5*	*Unclassifiable*
Severely ill	0	18	46	9	17	10
Mildly ill	2	21	57	6	3	11
Mean of ill groups	1	$19\frac{1}{2}$	$51\frac{1}{2}$	$7\frac{1}{2}$	10	$10\frac{1}{2}$
Normals	5	27	46	8	7	7

AGE:

	16–19	*20–9*	*30–9*	*40–9*	*50–9*	*60–9*	*70+*
Severely ill	1	31	28	21	12	5	2
Mildly ill	10	18	32	24	12	3	1
Mean of ill groups	$5\frac{1}{2}$	$24\frac{1}{2}$	30	$22\frac{1}{2}$	12	4	$1\frac{1}{2}$
Normals	5	23	26	25	13	7	1

APPENDIX 4

RESULTS OF THE ITEM ANALYSIS

* = Item accepted
(R) = Item rejected

ITEM	GROUP	REFUSED	1	2	3	4	GHQ SCORE
A.1							
* —feeling well	NORMAL	1	4	90	5	0	5
and in good	MILD	0	15	50	30	5	35
health?	SEVERE	0	16	22	40	23	63
A.2							
* —feeling in	NORMAL	0	67	27	6	0	6
need of good	MILD	4	25	41	24	6	30
tonic?	SEVERE	3	18	16	31	33	64
A.3							
* —run-down	NORMAL	1	64	28	7	0	7
and out of	MILD	1	17	41	37	4	41
sorts?	SEVERE	4	9	20	29	38	67
A.4							
* —felt that	NORMAL	1	85	9	5	0	5
you are ill?	MILD	1	32	40	22	5	27
	SEVERE	1	12	18	37	32	69
A.5							
(R) —worried	NORMAL	1	94	5	1	0	1
about losing	MILD	0	83	9	7	1	8
weight?	SEVERE	2	58	20	9	11	20
A.6							
(R) —putting on	NORMAL	0	64	28	6	2	8
too much	MILD	2	61	18	14	5	19
weight?	SEVERE	0	72	18	8	2	10
A.7							
* —getting any	NORMAL	0	75	22	2	1	3
pains in your	MILD	1	46	31	19	3	22
head?	SEVERE	1	35	21	28	15	43
A.8							
(R) —really bad	NORMAL	0	81	14	4	1	5
headaches?	MILD	0	60	18	18	4	22
	SEVERE	2	41	13	27	17	44
A.9							
(R) —noises in	NORMAL	0	93	4	2	1	3
your ears?	MILD	0	70	20	10	0	10
	SEVERE	2	65	14	17	2	19
A.10							
* —tightness or	NORMAL	0	91	8	1	0	1
pressure in	MILD	1	51	26	19	3	22
head?	SEVERE	1	42	17	28	12	40

ITEM	GROUP	REFUSED	1	2	3	4	GHQ SCORE
A.11							
* — couldn't give mind?	NORMAL	0	79	19	2	0	2
	MILD	0	26	43	21	10	31
	SEVERE	1	14	22	35	28	63
A.12							
(R) — pins and needles in hands and feet?	NORMAL	0	75	22	3	0	3
	MILD	1	73	12	13	1	14
	SEVERE	3	55	18	18	7	25
A.13							
* — hands shaking and trembling?	NORMAL	0	91	9	0	0	0
	MILD	0	57	28	13	2	15
	SEVERE	1	46	14	22	17	39
A.14							
* — bothered by noise?	NORMAL	0	58	40	2	0	2
	MILD	0	31	39	28	2	30
	SEVERE	1	27	27	31	13	44
A.15							
(R) — blushing easily?	NORMAL	0	69	29	2	0	2
	MILD	1	56	35	8	0	8
	SEVERE	3	54	36	7	0	7
A.16							
(R) — might have terrible disease?	NORMAL	0	93	6	1	0	1
	MILD	0	73	13	13	1	14
	SEVERE	1	62	12	15	9	24
A.17							
* — concentrate on whatever you are doing?	NORMAL	0	2	94	4	0	4
	MILD	0	13	42	35	10	45
	SEVERE	2	2	23	35	38	73
B.1							
(R) — worried about your heart?	NORMAL	0	92	7	1	0	1
	MILD	0	76	13	9	2	11
	SEVERE	2	68	11	14	5	19
B.2							
* — collapse in public place?	NORMAL	0	95	5	0	0	0
	MILD	1	58	20	15	6	21
	SEVERE	2	53	14	20	11	31
B.3							
(R) — aware of heart thumping?	NORMAL	0	85	14	1	0	1
	MILD	0	50	25	22	3	25
	SEVERE	2	41	25	21	11	32
B.4							
(R) — had any palpitations?	NORMAL	0	91	8	1	0	1
	MILD	4	58	28	10	0	10
	SEVERE	4	54	19	16	7	23
B.5							
(R) — frightened . . . heart suddenly stop?	NORMAL	0	92	7	1	0	1
	MILD	0	83	9	5	3	8
	SEVERE	0	73	13	6	8	14
B.6							
* — hot or cold spells?	NORMAL	0	81	17	2	0	2
	MILD	1	53	22	21	3	24
	SEVERE	2	32	15	31	20	51

ITEM	GROUP	REFUSED	1	2	3	4	GHQ SCORE
B.7							
* — *perspiring*	NORMAL	0	60	38	2	0	2
a lot?	MILD	0	38	37	20	5	25
	SEVERE	1	29	26	19	25	44
B.8							
(R) — *getting short*	NORMAL	1	59	36	4	0	4
of breath?	MILD	1	37	27	29	6	35
	SEVERE	0	46	24	16	14	30
B.9							
(R) — *suffered from*	NORMAL	0	59	31	7	3	10
backache?	MILD	1	55	24	17	3	20
	SEVERE	1	49	22	13	15	28
B.10							
(R) — *aches and*	NORMAL	0	50	40	10	0	10
pains in your	MILD	1	39	36	21	3	24
body?	SEVERE	3	32	26	24	15	39
B.11							
* — *been off your*	NORMAL	0	88	9	3	0	3
food?	MILD	2	54	22	21	1	22
	SEVERE	1	23	22	19	35	54
B.12							
(R) — *been feeling*	NORMAL	0	85	11	4	0	4
nauseated?	MILD	0	58	16	17	9	26
	SEVERE	1	44	15	26	14	40
B.13							
(R) — *been getting*	NORMAL	0	53	41	5	1	6
indigestion?	MILD	0	52	28	14	6	20
	SEVERE	1	51	20	19	9	28
B.14							
(R) — *food doing*	NORMAL	0	90	9	1	0	1
you no good?	MILD	0	74	15	7	4	11
	SEVERE	1	50	22	13	14	27
B.15							
(R) — *griping pains*	NORMAL	0	83	11	6	0	6
in belly?	MILD	1	69	18	8	4	12
	SEVERE	2	56	18	15	9	24
B.16							
(R) — *troubled by*	NORMAL	0	60	30	9	1	10
wind?	MILD	0	49	33	14	4	18
	SEVERE	0	52	20	20	8	28
B.17							
(R) — *any*	NORMAL	0	84	14	2	0	2
diarrhoea?	MILD	0	70	20	8	2	10
	SEVERE	3	63	7	21	6	27
B.18							
(R) — *suffered from*	NORMAL	1	72	26	1	0	1
constipation?	MILD	0	62	22	14	2	16
	SEVERE	2	45	22	17	14	31
C.1							
* — *waking early,*	NORMAL	0	67	28	5	0	5
unable to sleep?	MILD	1	46	27	16	10	26
	SEVERE	1	17	25	22	35	57

	ITEM	GROUP	REFUSED	1	2	3	4	GHQ SCORE
C.2								
*	— sleep hasn't	NORMAL	o	42	50	7	1	8
	refreshed?	MILD	o	17	49	21	14	35
		SEVERE	2	8	22	28	40	68
C.3								
*	— long time to	NORMAL	1	52	44	4	o	4
	get going?	MILD	o	16	46	26	12	38
		SEVERE	o	19	22	29	29	58
C.4								
*	— too tired	NORMAL	o	87	10	3	o	3
	to eat?	MILD	o	51	28	17	4	21
		SEVERE	o	32	19	26	23	49
C.5								
*	— lacking in	NORMAL	o	51	41	8	o	8
	energy?	MILD	o	16	42	30	12	42
		SEVERE	2	8	19	37	34	71
C.6								
*	— lost sleep	NORMAL	o	74	24	2	o	2
	over worry?	MILD	o	36	34	21	9	30
		SEVERE	1	10	18	32	39	71
C.7								
*	— mentally alert	NORMAL	o	3	93	4	o	4
	and wide awake?	MILD	o	8	53	35	4	39
		SEVERE	1	12	28	33	26	59
C.8								
*	— full of	NORMAL	o	8	82	10	o	10
	energy?	MILD	o	3	47	35	15	50
		SEVERE	2	3	16	35	44	79
C.9								
*	— restless and	NORMAL	o	48	46	6	o	6
	unable to	MILD	1	9	38	36	16	52
	relax?	SEVERE	1	7	20	29	43	72
C.10								
*	— easily	NORMAL	o	42	47	11	o	11
	fatigued?	MILD	1	10	41	37	11	48
		SEVERE	2	10	24	28	36	64
C.11								
*	— spells of	NORMAL	o	81	18	1	o	1
	exhaustion?	MILD	1	42	27	24	6	30
		SEVERE	1	32	23	21	23	44
C.12								
(R)	— too tired	NORMAL	o	47	41	12	o	12
	in evenings . . .	MILD	o	20	43	28	9	37
	sit?	SEVERE	1	13	30	28	28	56
C.13								
*	— tired and	NORMAL	o	44	47	9	o	9
	ready for	MILD	o	26	36	31	7	38
	bed?	SEVERE	o	18	25	27	30	57
C.14								
*	— difficulty	NORMAL	o	66	29	5	o	5
	getting to	MILD	1	40	27	24	8	32
	sleep?	SEVERE	1	16	21	25	37	62

	ITEM	GROUP	REFUSED	I	2	3	4	GHQ SCORE
C.15								
*	— sleeping	NORMAL	o	92	8	o	o	o
	pills?	MILD	o	61	23	6	10	16
		SEVERE	3	30	16	13	38	51
C.16								
*	— staying	NORMAL	o	85	13	2	o	2
	asleep?	MILD	I	52	23	19	5	24
		SEVERE	o	30	20	24	26	50
C.17								
*	— unpleasant	NORMAL	o	83	16	I	o	I
	dreams?	MILD	I	38	34	25	2	27
		SEVERE	2	31	26	13	28	51
C.18								
(R)	— getting up	NORMAL	I	65	31	3	o	3
	to pass water?	MILD	3	56	30	9	2	11
		SEVERE	o	42	31	15	12	27
C.19								
*	— restless and	NORMAL	o	74	25	I	o	I
	disturbed nights?	MILD	o	37	33	22	8	30
		SEVERE	I	16	26	26	31	57
D.1								
(R)	— giving vent	NORMAL	o	72	24	3	I	4
	to feelings?	MILD	o	55	20	17	8	25
		SEVERE	o	51	19	17	13	30
D.2								
*	— on the brink	NORMAL	o	63	29	7	I	8
	of tears?	MILD	o	18	35	32	15	47
		SEVERE	o	9	17	30	44	74
D.3								
*	— given way	NORMAL	o	78	21	I	o	I
	to tears?	MILD	o	44	21	21	14	35
		SEVERE	o	27	12	24	37	61
D.4								
*	— keep busy	NORMAL	o	29	69	2	o	2
	and occupied?	MILD	I	13	57	24	5	29
		SEVERE	I	7	29	24	39	63
D.5								
(R)	—having to	NORMAL	o	9	88	2	I	3
	do things	MILD	I	11	70	11	7	18
	repeatedly?	SEVERE	3	15	54	13	15	28
D.6								
*	— putting things	NORMAL	o	32	59	8	I	9
	off?	MILD	o	21	37	35	7	42
		SEVERE	2	8	29	28	33	61
D.7								
*	— taking longer	NORMAL	o	6	87	6	I	7
	over things?	MILD	o	7	56	27	10	37
		SEVERE	I	5	37	27	30	57
D.8								
*	— lose interest?	NORMAL	o	60	31	9	o	9
		MILD	I	22	34	34	9	43
		SEVERE	2	11	16	33	38	71

ITEM	GROUP	REFUSED	I	2	3	4	GHQ SCORE
D.9							
* — sit about	NORMAL	0	55	37	7	1	8
doing	MILD	0	31	29	30	10	40
nothing?	SEVERE	0	22	19	23	36	59
D.10							
* — losing	NORMAL	0	77	17	5	1	6
interest . . .	MILD	0	54	24	19	3	22
appearance?	SEVERE	1	26	23	21	29	50
D.11							
* — less trouble	NORMAL	0	8	85	5	2	7
with clothes?	MILD	0	9	68	16	7	23
	SEVERE	1	11	42	21	25	46
D.12							
(R) — biting your	NORMAL	2	67	27	3	1	4
nails?	MILD	0	55	27	13	5	18
	SEVERE	0	49	18	16	17	33
D.13							
* — getting out	NORMAL	0	13	77	7	3	10
of house?	MILD	0	8	64	17	11	28
	SEVERE	2	14	25	22	37	59
D.14							
(R) — going out in	NORMAL	0	12	70	10	8	18
evenings . . .	MILD	0	6	43	31	20	51
enjoy?	SEVERE	0	9	25	21	45	66
D.15							
(R) — able to go	NORMAL	1	2	94	1	2	3
into shops?	MILD	0	11	71	10	8	18
	SEVERE	0	3	65	10	22	32
D.16							
(R) — afraid to go	NORMAL	0	96	4	0	0	0
out alone	MILD	0	69	20	12	9	21
	SEVERE	0	54	16	11	10	21
D.17							
* — managing as	NORMAL	0	24	75	1	0	1
well as most	MILD	1	21	54	19	5	24
people?	SEVERE	3	12	44	21	20	41
D.18							
* — doing things	NORMAL	0	8	87	5	0	5
well?	MILD	1	10	57	23	9	32
	SEVERE	1	3	38	24	34	58
D.19							
* — time off	NORMAL	2	74	21	3	0	3
work?	MILD	5	39	27	20	9	29
	SEVERE	3	23	16	23	35	58
D.20							
* — late to	NORMAL	0	65	34	1	0	1
work?	MILD	8	35	29	21	7	28
	SEVERE	7	30	17	21	25	46
D.21							
* — difficulty	NORMAL	1	10	85	4	0	4
keeping up?	MILD	7	9	51	26	7	33
	SEVERE	1	7	24	30	38	68

ITEM		GROUP	REFUSED	1	2	3	4	GHQ SCORE
D.22								
* — satisfied		NORMAL	0	9	87	4	0	4
with task?		MILD	4	6	59	26	5	31
		SEVERE	2	5	34	26	33	59
E.1								
* — worried		NORMAL	1	54	39	6	0	6
about		MILD	0	10	28	44	18	62
effect on?		SEVERE	0	11	17	23	49	72
E.2								
(R) — getting on		NORMAL	0	19	76	3	2	5
well with those		MILD	0	15	53	25	7	32
close?		SEVERE	0	4	53	15	28	43
E.3								
(R) — feel warmth		NORMAL	0	20	76	2	2	4
and affection?		MILD	1	16	52	19	12	31
		SEVERE	1	19	37	20	23	43
E.4								
(R) — what is		NORMAL	0	19	59	17	5	22
going to		MILD	1	10	37	32	20	52
happen to . . .?		SEVERE	1	11	17	28	43	71
E.5								
(R) — losing		NORMAL	0	37	56	7	0	7
temper?		MILD	0	28	30	32	10	42
		SEVERE	0	36	22	20	22	42
E.6								
* — feeling that		NORMAL	0	84	15	1	0	1
you're a		MILD	0	20	40	24	16	40
burden?		SEVERE	0	18	13	33	36	69
E.7								
(R) — on your		NORMAL	0	75	23	2	0	2
guard even		MILD	3	38	36	18	5	23
with friends?		SEVERE	1	33	26	22	18	40
E.8								
(R) — getting		NORMAL	0	12	86	2	0	2
on well with		MILD	4	8	71	16	1	17
friends?		SEVERE	0	9	62	14	15	29
E.9								
(R) — all right		NORMAL	0	4	96	0	0	0
with		MILD	7	5	80	6	2	8
neighbours?		SEVERE	3	5	71	9	12	21
E.10								
(R) — easy to get		NORMAL	0	13	86	1	0	1
on with other		MILD	2	6	74	13	5	18
people?		SEVERE	0	6	58	20	16	36
E.11								
* — spent time		NORMAL	0	15	77	7	1	8
chatting?		MILD	2	13	59	14	12	26
		SEVERE	0	16	33	23	28	51
E.12								
(R) — others		NORMAL	0	38	39	17	6	23
regard you as		MILD	2	16	27	43	12	55
touchy?		SEVERE	3	21	19	39	18	57

ITEM	GROUP	REFUSED	1	2	3	4	GHQ SCORE
E.13 * — need to talk to others?	NORMAL	0	17	74	9	0	9
	MILD	1	13	44	25	17	42
	SEVERE	1	14	28	27	30	57
E.14 * — afraid to say anything in case . . .?	NORMAL	0	72	26	2	0	2
	MILD	2	25	55	16	2	18
	SEVERE	0	28	29	24	19	53
E.15 * — others seem to have misunderstood?	NORMAL	0	49	49	2	0	2
	MILD	2	29	50	16	3	19
	SEVERE	1	22	35	24	18	42
E.16 * — brooding over things . . . people?	NORMAL	0	67	31	2	0	2
	MILD	2	15	45	28	10	38
	SEVERE	0	24	29	23	24	47
E.17 * — others getting on your nerves?	NORMAL	0	51	42	7	0	7
	MILD	2	15	41	31	11	42
	SEVERE	0	20	26	30	24	54
E.18 (R) — difficulty speaking to strangers?	NORMAL	1	64	34	1	0	1
	MILD	3	43	39	9	6	15
	SEVERE	0	35	30	16	19	35
E.19 (R) — properly valued by others?	NORMAL	1	10	86	1	2	3
	MILD	1	6	69	18	6	24
	SEVERE	4	9	55	15	17	32
E.20 * — no good to anybody?	NORMAL	1	71	24	3	1	4
	MILD	0	29	38	21	12	33
	SEVERE	1	19	13	27	40	67
F.1 * — playing a useful part?	NORMAL	2	13	80	4	1	5
	MILD	2	5	51	32	10	42
	SEVERE	1	5	25	33	36	69
F.2 (R) — contented with your lot?	NORMAL	2	16	63	14	5	19
	MILD	1	4	35	39	21	60
	SEVERE	3	7	21	24	45	69
F.3 * — capable of making decisions?	NORMAL	1	12	84	3	0	3
	MILD	1	11	55	26	7	33
	SEVERE	1	7	27	30	35	65
F.4 * — not able to make start?	NORMAL	1	64	30	5	0	5
	MILD	0	21	50	25	4	29
	SEVERE	1	16	24	32	27	59
F.5 * — dreading things you have to do?	NORMAL	1	76	21	2	0	2
	MILD	0	31	35	28	6	34
	SEVERE	1	21	22	26	30	56

	ITEM	GROUP	REFUSED	I	2	3	4	GHQ SCORE
F.6								
★	— constantly	NORMAL	I	61	32	6	0	6
	under strain?	MILD	0	9	45	34	12	46
		SEVERE	2	7	18	27	46	73
F.7								
★	— couldn't	NORMAL	I	68	28	3	0	3
	overcome	MILD	I	12	45	29	13	42
	difficulties?	SEVERE	3	8	16	26	47	73
F.8								
★	— afraid . . .	NORMAL	I	69	27	3	0	3
	express foolish	MILD	0	32	43	20	5	25
	mistakes?	SEVERE	I	21	22	25	31	56
F.9								
★	— frightened	NORMAL	I	87	11	I	0	I
	to be on	MILD	0	54	26	10	10	20
	your own?	SEVERE	0	35	19	19	27	46
F.10								
★	— confident	NORMAL	I	6	92	I	0	I
	about public	MILD	0	9	64	22	5	27
	places?	SEVERE	I	4	53	21	21	42
F.11								
(R)	— afraid of	NORMAL	0	96	4	0	0	0
	papers, TV	MILD	I	76	15	3	4	7
	because . . .?	SEVERE	0	56	23	12	9	21
F.12								
(R)	— as though	NORMAL	0	84	14	I	I	2
	you were not	MILD	2	48	23	22	5	27
	really there?	SEVERE	2	42	20	21	15	36
F.13								
★	— finding life	NORMAL	0	58	39	3	0	3
	a struggle?	MILD	I	15	40	36	8	44
		SEVERE	0	9	26	30	35	65
F.14								
★	— blaming	NORMAL	I	50	43	6	0	6
	yourself . . .	MILD	I	14	52	24	9	33
	things go wrong?	SEVERE	0	12	25	27	36	63
F.15								
★	— enjoy normal	NORMAL	0	12	84	4	0	4
	day activities?	MILD	I	6	44	38	11	49
		SEVERE	0	3	28	26	43	69
F.16								
★	— taking things	NORMAL	0	52	45	3	0	3
	hard?	MILD	3	16	41	28	12	40
		SEVERE	3	11	17	32	37	69
F.17								
★	— edgy and	NORMAL	0	37	54	9	0	9
	bad tempered?	MILD	0	17	35	32	16	48
		SEVERE	2	18	26	34	20	54
F.18								
★	— scared and	NORMAL	0	80	19	I	0	I
	panicky . . . no	MILD	I	20	43	24	12	36
	reason?	SEVERE	I	18	20	31	30	61

ITEM		GROUP	REFUSED	I	2	3	4	GHQ SCORE
F.19								
★	— able to	NORMAL	0	8	90	2	0	2
	face your	MILD	I	6	55	25	13	38
	problems?	SEVERE	0	5	22	33	40	73
F.20								
(R)	— worry over	NORMAL	0	26	55	19	0	19
	money?	MILD	I	25	40	23	II	34
		SEVERE	I	29	32	13	25	38
F.21								
★	— everything	NORMAL	0	48	47	5	0	5
	on top of you?	MILD	0	18	33	31	18	49
		SEVERE	2	6	20	28	44	72
F.22								
(R)	— easily	NORMAL	0	47	38	15	0	15
	upset over	MILD	I	10	37	33	19	52
	things?	SEVERE	0	9	21	34	36	70
F.23								
(R)	— little annoy-	NORMAL	0	45	43	12	0	12
	ances, upset	MILD	I	17	32	34	15	49
	and angry?	SEVERE	0	16	29	30	25	55
F.24								
★	— people	NORMAL	0	65	34	I	0	I
	looking at	MILD	I	49	35	12	3	15
	you?	SEVERE	0	30	29	27	14	41
F.25								
★	— feelings	NORMAL	0	44	51	5	0	5
	easily hurt?	MILD	0	13	44	34	9	43
		SEVERE	0	II	23	35	31	66
G.I								
★	— feeling	NORMAL	0	56	35	9	0	9
	unhappy and	MILD	I	9	32	37	20	57
	depressed?	SEVERE	2	0	13	28	58	86
G.2								
★	— losing	NORMAL	0	70	23	7	0	7
	confidence in	MILD	0	16	40	29	15	44
	yourself?	SEVERE	0	5	17	25	53	78
G.3								
★	— thinking of	NORMAL	0	77	18	5	0	5
	yourself as	MILD	I	33	33	24	9	33
	worthless?	SEVERE	0	12	14	23	5I	74
G.4								
★	— life entirely	NORMAL	0	84	12	4	0	4
	hopeless?	MILD	I	40	31	17	II	28
		SEVERE	0	17	17	20	46	66
G.5								
★	— hopeful about	NORMAL	0	19	75	4	2	6
	your future?	MILD	I	12	4I	29	17	46
		SEVERE	I	II	29	15	44	59
G.6								
★	— reasonably	NORMAL	0	18	72	5	0	5
	happy?	MILD	0	14	37	36	12	58
		SEVERE	I	7	24	27	4I	68

ITEM	GROUP	REFUSED	1	2	3	4	GHQ SCORE
G.7 * — *worrying unduly?*	NORMAL	0	60	34	6	0	6
	MILD	0	14	47	28	10	38
	SEVERE	0	20	24	31	25	56
G.8 * — *afraid you might be losing control?*	NORMAL	0	86	11	2	1	3
	MILD	0	33	27	30	10	40
	SEVERE	0	16	21	31	32	63
G.9 * — *afraid something awful is going to happen?*	NORMAL	0	81	15	4	0	4
	MILD	0	29	36	23	12	35
	SEVERE	0	21	19	22	38	60
G.10 * — *going to have a nervous breakdown?*	NORMAL	0	89	8	3	0	3
	MILD	1	26	41	19	14	33
	SEVERE	2	23	24	17	34	51
G.11 * — *feeling nervous and strung up all the time?*	NORMAL	1	66	27	6	0	6
	MILD	0	9	43	32	16	48
	SEVERE	1	8	19	25	47	72
G.12 (R) — *anxious someone may have been harmed?*	NORMAL	1	67	27	5	0	5
	MILD	1	45	29	16	9	25
	SEVERE	5	38	22	13	22	35
G.13 * — *felt that life isn't worth living?*	NORMAL	1	87	10	2	0	2
	MILD	1	40	28	19	12	31
	SEVERE	2	18	20	19	41	60
G.14 * — *possibility that you might make away with yourself?*	NORMAL	1	85	6	7	1	8
	MILD	1	41	14	29	15	44
	SEVERE	1	29	11	21	38	59
G.15 * — *couldn't do anything because nerves were too bad?*	NORMAL	1	91	8	0	0	0
	MILD	0	32	34	24	10	34
	SEVERE	1	13	22	21	43	64
G.16 * — *thoughts going round and round certain things?*	NORMAL	1	41	47	9	2	11
	MILD	0	10	34	41	15	56
	SEVERE	0	5	12	39	44	83
G.17 * — *unwelcome thoughts keep coming in?*	NORMAL	1	64	30	5	0	5
	MILD	0	17	41	26	16	42
	SEVERE	0	21	16	27	36	63
G.18 * — *wishing you were dead and away from it all?*	NORMAL	1	92	6	1	0	1
	MILD	1	42	29	15	13	28
	SEVERE	2	26	18	13	41	54

ITEM	GROUP	REFUSED	1	2	3	4	GHQ SCORE
G.19							
* — the idea of	NORMAL	1	90	5	3	1	4
taking your own	MILD	3	43	18	21	15	36
life kept coming	SEVERE	1	34	8	21	36	57
into your mind?							

H.1

		REFUSED	1	2	3	4
How tiring did	NORMAL	1	88	8	2	1
you find this	MILD	1	49	34	14	2
questionnaire?	SEVERE	2	33	30	17	18

Key:
1 = No bother at all.
2 = Tired, but accurate.
3 = Tired towards the end and may not have been accurate.
4 = Very tiring. Many of the items difficult.

H.2

		REFUSED	1	2	3	4	5
Do you think	NORMAL	2	27	71	0	0	0
that you are	MILD	1	4	26	41	27	1
at all ill?	SEVERE	4	2	13	27	46	8

Key:
1 = Healthier and more stable than average.
2 = About average.
3 = Slightly more nervous or ill than average.
4 = Fairly ill: would be helped by medical treatment.
5 = Very ill: need to be in hospital.

SOME SHORT CASE-HISTORIES EXEMPLIFYING THE VARIOUS GRADES OF PSYCHIATRIC ILLNESS DETECTED BY THE STANDARDIZED PSYCHIATRIC INTERVIEW

METHOD OF SELECTING THESE PARTICULAR VIGNETTES

The 200 completed interview schedules were divided into the five clinical categories representing each of five 'psychiatric severity ratings'. These were: psychiatrically normal (0), subclinical psychiatric disturbance (1), mild (2), moderate (3), and marked (4) psychiatric cases. Each of these five categories was then divided into male and female, making a total of 10 categories.

One case-history was then selected from each pile using random number tables to choose each one. It must be emphasized that no selection of any kind has been made concerning the 10 vignettes that now follow.

Vignette of Case No. 238. An example of a psychiatrically 'normal' patient (male)

Presenting complaint:

Mr. A. A. was a 69-year-old man who had come up to see the GP because he had a perpetual cold for the past 6 months. He denied being run-down—'quite the reverse doctor'—and had indeed been getting about far more, and feeling better, since a bilateral arthroplasty to the hips the previous year.

His previous health had been good apart from his osteo-arthritis.

Semistructured interview:

		RATING
Somatic symptoms:	Occasional heartburn and rheumatism unrelated to worry	1
Fatigue:	Occasional fatigue during day necessitating a rest	2
Sleep disturbance:	Takes an hour to drop off each night	1
Irritability:	None	0
Lack of concentration:	None	0
Depression:	None	0
Anxiety and worry:	None	0
Phobias:	None	0
Obsessions, etc.:	None, likes to be thorough	0
Depersonalization:	None	0

Manifest abnormalities:

None were observed

Formulation:

No psychiatric abnormalities detected. Longstanding coryza, possibly a sensitivity phenomenon, in an old man with osteo-arthritis.

Psychiatric diagnosis:

None was made
Overall severity rating: 'o' normal

Extract from the general practitioner's daybook:

Complaint: Osteo-arthritis of the hip
Diagnostic category: Entirely physical illness
Psychiatric severity rating: 'o' normal

GHQ Score: 6

Vignette of Case No. 70. An example of a psychiatrically 'normal' patient (female)

Presenting complaint:

Mrs. B. B. was a 57-year-old housewife who complained that her face was puffy around the eyes. In her past history she had had ankylosing spondylitis and a hysterectomy. At the age of 7 she was said to have had a 'nervous breakdown' at the time of an ear abscess.

Semistructured interview:		RATING
Somatic symptoms:	Intermittent backache, no relation to worry, etc.	I
Fatigue:	Tired out in the evenings, but works 16 hours a day!	I
Sleep disturbance:	None	o
Irritability:	Has always been rather irritable over trivialities	I
Lack of concentration:	None	o
Depression:	None	o
Anxiety and worry:	Always highly strung, occasional worries over mother's health	I
Phobias:	None	o
Obsessions, etc.:	Checks gas-taps, car-locks, etc. No struggle or distress	I
Depersonalization:	Occasional feelings of unreality while driving at night, but no unpleasant quality	I

Manifest abnormalities:

None were elicited or observed

Formulation:

On her history the coarseness of her skin and constantly feeling cold together with the puffiness of her face would make one want to exclude myxoedema. But her pulse was 80 and she had no other signs. Otherwise possibly a sensitivity phenomenon.

Psychiatric diagnosis:

None was made
Overall severity rating: 'o' normal

Extract from general practitioner's daybook:

Complaint:	Allergy
Diagnostic category:	Entirely physical illness
Psychiatric severity rating:	'o' normal

GHQ Score: 4

Vignette of Case No. 197. An example of a subclinical psychiatric disturbance
   (male)

Presenting complaint:

   Mr. C. C. was a 21-year-old engineering student who lived at home with his
parents. He had hurt his chest in the gymnasium that day, and had already been
to two doctors who had reassured him that all was well. But he still had some pain,
and knew a girl who had been accused of putting on her chest pain, but afterwards
turned out to have had a hole in her heart. Thus the third consultation that day!

Semistructured interview: RATING

Somatic symptoms:	The chest pain is clearly related to a strain while weight-lifting	o
Fatigue:	'I never feel tired'	o
Sleep disturbance:	Had lost a small amount of sleep in the previous week thinking about his 21st birthday party	I
Irritability:	None	o
Lack of concentration:	'I daydream a lot while I should be working —I'm not very bright you know'	I
Depression:	Mildly elated with new girl-friend	o
Anxiety and worry:	None (denies anxiety about chest pain!)	o
Phobias:	Dislikes it if alone in house at night	I
Obsessions, etc.:	None	o
Depersonalization:	None	o

Manifest abnormalities at interview:

ELATED, euphoric	A restless ball of energy. Bubbling over with high spirits and cheerfulness, but not clinically hypomanic	I
EXCESSIVE CONCERN WITH BODILY FUNCTIONS	Three consultations in I day for this pain— but seems to have accepted reassurance now	I

Formulation:

   A very active, cheerful lad who never feels tired and volunteers that he is happier
than most people. Amused by interview, talks loudly and pulls many faces while
describing himself. His impending 21st birthday is a great event for such an extro-
vert, and this, together with the obviously distorted story about the girl he knew,
probably accounts for his odd consulting behaviour today.

Psychiatric diagnosis:
   Hyperthymic personality
   Mild transient anxiety reaction (ICD 307—transient situational disturbance)
   Overall severity rating: '1' subclinical disturbance

Extract from general practitioner's daybook:

Complaint:	Pain in chest (effort syndrome)
Diagnostic category:	Psychiatric illness with somatic symptoms
Psychiatric severity rating:	'1' subclinical disturbance

GHQ Score: 2

Vignette of Case No. 120. An example of a subclinical psychiatric disturbance (female)

Presenting complaint:

   Mrs. D. D. was a 71-year-old housewife married to a retired engineer. She complained of mouth ulcers. She had had crops of them for many years, and was now having a particularly bad crop. She treated herself for her constipation, indigestion, and sinus headaches, but needed a prescription for the ulcers. In her past history she had once had shingles.

Semistructured interview: RATING

Somatic symptoms:	She lost the use of her arms and legs after her shingles and still gets neckaches that she attributes to this.	
	Many other aches and pains, and ulcers seem to be exacerbated by worry in case they're cancerous	2
Fatigue:	Occasionally feels tired, but soon recovers	1
Sleep disturbance:	Reads herself asleep by 2.00 a.m.	1
Irritability:	A bit snappy with the ulcers	1
Lack of concentration:	None	0
Depression:	None	0
Anxiety and worry:	Been worrying about her ulcers, and whether the shingles will return and she'll lose the use of her legs	
	Occasional in past week	2
Phobias:	None	0
Obsessions, etc.:	None	0
Depersonalization:	None	0

Manifest abnormalities at interview:

DEPRESSED	Mild, subclinical in intensity	1
ANXIOUS	Mild, subclinical in intensity	1
EXCESSIVE CONCERN WITH BODILY FUNCTIONS	Very difficult rating problem, but on the whole her fear that her ulcers may be cancerous is not strongly held or totally unreasonable	1

Formulation:

An otherwise well-adjusted, intelligent old lady who has many physical symptoms. Each of them *could* be organic. She is clearly on the borderline between being a case and not being one, but one lacks enough definite data. Her fear that her aphthous ulcers may be cancerous is hardly justified, since she has had crops of them all her life. The paralysis after the herpes doesn't sound organic.

Psychiatric diagnosis:

Possible mild affective illness with somatic symptoms—*subclinical*
Overall severity rating: '1' subclinical disturbance

Extract from general practitioner's daybook:

Complaint: Mouth ulcers, minor affective illness
Diagnostic category: Unrelated physical and psychiatric conditions
Psychiatric severity rating: '2' a mild psychiatric case

GHQ Score: 3

Vignette of Case No. 432. An example of a mild psychiatric case (male)

Presenting complaint:

Mr. E. E. was a 22-year-old communications engineer who still lived with his parents prior to his forthcoming marriage. He presented with a sore throat that he had had for 2 days, but on inquiry also described severe headaches that he had been having for the past 2 months. They were worse in the evenings, bifrontal and accompanied by nausea.

Semistructured interview:		RATING
Somatic symptoms:	His headaches seemed related to his doubts about his forthcoming marriage; very distressing and severe	3
Fatigue:	Constantly listless for previous 5 months	3
Sleep disturbance:	None	0
Irritability:	Occasional flare-ups with father Unlike him	2
Lack of concentration:	Can no longer do things as well as he used; everything takes longer, hard to concentrate, frequent	3
Depression:	Has felt down in dumps and fed-up in previous week	2
Anxiety and worry:	Had occasional anxiety feelings for no reason in previous week. Worried about marriage and looking for house	2
Phobias:	None	0
Obsessions, etc.:	Checks × 3, no struggle, not distressing Habitually indecisive	1
Depersonalization:	None	0

Manifest abnormalities at interview: RATING

ANXIOUS   Clearly anxious and indecisive about the
major decisions looming ahead. Very glad
to have opportunity to discuss his doubts
and worries with a doctor   2

DEPRESSED   Gloomy rather than depressed (depression
subclinical)   1

EXCESSIVE CONCERN WITH   Has cut down his smoking to 20/day because
    BODILY FUNCTIONS   he has recently begun to worry about cancer   1

Formulation:

A neat young man with a long orderly row of multicoloured biros sticking out of his pocket: he has always needed to ask others to help him with decisions, and has derived pleasure from checking and rechecking his work. After a 5-year courtship he has finally made the decision to marry, but this seems to have been at the cost of a mild anxiety state. He was visibly relieved to have had a chance to discuss his doubts today.

Psychiatric diagnosis:

    Mild anxiety state. Engyesis
    Obsessional personality
    (ICD 300.0—anxiety neurosis; 301.4—anancastic personality)
    Overall severity rating: '2' mild psychiatric illness

Extract from the general practitioner's daybook:

Complaint: Sore throat (minor affective syndrome; engyesis)
Diagnostic category: Psychiatric illness with somatic symptoms
Psychiatric severity rating: '1' subclinical disturbance
GHQ Score: 21

Vignette of Case No. 21. An example of a mild psychiatric case (female)

Presenting complaint:

Miss F. F. was a 20-year-old girl who had broken off her engagement 2 months previously, very much against her parents' wishes. She had felt ill ever since that time, and 5 days before had developed 'piles and an anal infection'. She had also lost some weight, and was having dysmenorrhoea.

Semistructured interview: RATING

Somatic symptoms: Bad headache every evening in past week,
related to problems   3
Fatigue: Fatigue every day, having to go to bed early   3
Sleep disturbance: Lost 1 night's sleep with headache   2
Irritability: Snappy with people at work. Unusual for her   2
Lack of concentration: Can't concentrate on a book, getting
forgetful at home, knocks into things,
difficulty of concentration causing
difficulties with her boss   3
Depression: Occasional weeping spells in past week
related to broken engagement   2

		RATING
Anxiety and worry:	Worries a little about what others think of her	I
Phobias:	Frightened of dark and going out at night	I
Obsessions, etc.:	None	o
Depersonalization:	None	o

Manifest abnormalities at interview:

DEPRESSED	She appears clinically depressed in mild degree	2

Formulation:

Her headache, malaise, loss of weight, fatigue and irritability are all part of a minor affective illness that has followed her decision to break off her engagement. She has felt depressed and had periods of weeping during this time.

Psychiatric diagnosis:

Mild depression. Overall severity rating: '2'
(ICD 300.4—depressive neurosis)

Extract from the general practitioner's daybook:

Complaint:	Ischiorectal abscess. Recent engyesis
Diagnostic category:	Unrelated psychiatric and physical illnesses
Psychiatric severity rating:	'2' mild psychiatric case

GHQ Score: 26

Vignette of Case No. 246. An example of a moderate psychiatric case (**male**)

Presenting complaint:

Mr. G. G. was a 45-year-old examiner in bankruptcy who had attended his GP because of a sudden feeling that a big cloud had come down on him. This odd, and unpleasant, feeling was accompanied by a constant headache and a feeling of heaviness in his eyes. He felt constantly on the verge of tears. He depicted himself as a cyclothymic personality who had had no previous attacks of this sort, although after the death of his father when he was a boy of 10 he had developed a bad stutter that had persisted for some years.

Semistructured interview:

		RATING
Somatic symptoms:	Frequent distressing headache, came on at the same time as other symptoms, accompanied by stiffness of neck	3
Fatigue:	Occasional feelings of fatigue	2
Sleep disturbance:	Distressing nightmares antedated symptoms, but none in previous week	o
Irritability:	Occasional bursts of irritability at home and in office	2
Lack of concentration:	Has noticed difficulties in concentrating in previous week	2
Depression:	Constant feeling of depression, on verge of tears	3

		RATING
Anxiety and worry:	Constant worry over his job in previous week	3
Phobias:	Occasionally feels claustrophobic at home, not in past week	1
Obsessions, etc.:	None	0
Depersonalization:	None	0

Manifest abnormalities at interview:

DEPRESSED	He has a clinically significant depression of mood of moderate degree	3
ANXIOUS, tense	He is noticeably tense at interview, and his headache and stiff neck suggest that this has lasted for some days	2
DEPRESSIVE THOUGHT CONTENT	Although he is not suicidal at present he has chosen the gas-taps at home as what he would use for his suicide	2
EXCESSIVE CONCERN WITH BODILY FUNCTIONS	Very worried about his smoking, more than 20/day—this worry has begun recently (Non-morbid rating assigned for this)	1

Formulation:

An intelligent man who gives a clear and convincing account of a depressive illness. He describes a cyclothymic personality, and notes that a period of mild elation which had lasted nearly 4 months ended 7 days ago. He has been under considerable strain at work for some time. The present episode has a number of features that distinguish it from his usual depressive swings of mood. It was ushered in by a number of nightmares of coffins and corpses, and has been accompanied by many somatic symptoms of anxiety. The depressive mood itself is unlike his usual feelings of gloominess reactive to external circumstances, but is a pervasive heavy feeling as described above.

Psychiatric diagnosis:

Affective illness: depression
(ICD diagnosis: 296.2—manic-depressive psychosis, depressed type)
Overall severity rating: '3'

Extract from the general practitioner's daybook:

Complaint:	Depression: manic personality
Diagnostic category:	Entirely psychiatric condition
Psychiatric severity rating:	'3' moderate psychiatric illness

GHQ Score: 19

Vignette of Case No. 438. An example of a moderate psychiatric case (female)

Presenting complaint:

Mrs. H. H. was a 45-year-old housewife who did voluntary work at a clinic. She had come to see the doctor about a sore throat she had had for 2 weeks, but having filled up the questionnaire she remarked to the doctor after he had examined her throat that 'most of my troubles are on that form'. She wanted to tell someone about her 'black moods'. During these she says wounding things to her husband and goes silent in company and with her family. Her moods last for weeks at a time. In her past history she had had a hysterectomy 5 years ago and had needed 'nerve pills' for a time after this.

Semistructured interview:		RATING
Somatic symptoms:	None	0
Fatigue:	Occasional fatigue during day, 'can't be bothered'	2
Sleep disturbance:	None	0
Irritability:	This has been constant and involved everyone	3
Lack of concentration:	She can no longer concentrate on her housework, read books, or do crosswords or concentrate on TV. Constant	3
Depression:	Constant feeling of depression: 'Nothing pushes away the evil blackness in my mind.' Feels completely hopeless Tempted to drive her car at 60 mph into a tree last week	3
Anxiety and worry:	Occasional mild worry, nothing serious	1
Phobias:	None	0
Obsessions, etc.:	Loathsome thoughts about husband come into her mind against her will, very distressing, can't get rid of them. During this time she folds and refolds towels in the bathroom, compelled to keep doing this over and over. Quite unlike herself usually	3
Depersonalization:	None	0

Manifest abnormalities at interview:

DEPRESSED	Clinically significant depression of mild degree	2
DEPRESSIVE THOUGHTS	Thinks everything is her fault, sees no future	2
EXCESSIVE CONCERN WITH BODILY FUNCTIONS	Afraid that her sore throat is due to cancer of throat (accepts reassurance)	2

Formulation:

A rather neurotic personality, whose depressive fluctuations in mood seem to be connected with strongly held ideas that she has about the importance of living in a larger house: this was clinically an overvalued idea. Her present depression has many minor obsessional features.

Psychiatric diagnosis:

Affective illness: depression with obsessional features
(ICD diagnosis: 300.4—depressive neurosis)
Overall severity rating: '3' moderate psychiatric case

Extract from the general practitioner's daybook:

Complaint:	Sore throat; affective illness
Diagnostic category:	Unrelated physical and psychiatric diagnoses
Psychiatric severity rating:	'3' moderate psychiatric case

GHQ Score: 37

Vignette of Case No. 609. An example of a marked psychiatric case (male)

Presenting complaint:

Mr. I. I. was a 34-year-old reinsurance broker who had developed what he described as 'paranoid symptoms' while on a business trip in South America. He began to attribute special meanings to trivial things he saw, and heard voices discussing him in Spanish during the night. He became convinced that his Panamanian business colleagues were trying to murder him, and also that he had somehow caught tetanus. While fleeing from his persecutors he was befriended by a prostitute and was convinced that he had caught syphilis, and on returning home he went to his mother's home rather than back to his wife and children. He arranged to call home while his wife was out, and became convinced that she had been unfaithful to him while he had been away.

Semistructured interview: RATING

Somatic symptoms:	None	0
Fatigue:	None	0
Sleep disturbance:	Occasional nightmares, dreams of violence, no loss of sleep	1
Irritability:	Occasionally irritable with wife, feels that she's nagging	2
Lack of concentration:	None	0
Depression:	Felt constantly depressed, occasionally hopeless	3
Anxiety and worry:	Constant extreme anxiety about VD and secondary to his delusions	4
Phobias:	Worried in case he's left alone in house, but hasn't been	1
Obsessions, etc.:	Has been checking his work × 2 although he knows that it's right, struggles and is distressed by this. Thoughts that he is really a homosexual come into his mind against his will	2
Depersonalization:	None	0

Manifest abnormalities at interview:

DELUSIONS	Believes that he has tetanus and VD, does not accept reassurance. Still believes that he was being plotted against in various South American countries	3
DEPRESSIVE THOUGHTS	Feels that he is undoubtedly inferior to others—'it has a sound basis, I'm objectively limited compared with others' Also has ideas of self-blame	3
ANXIOUS, AGITATED	Very tense and agitated as he gives history and describes how he has felt about recent events	3
EXCESSIVE CONCERN WITH BODILY FUNCTIONS	Constantly preoccupied with idea that he has VD, is also worried about his mental health	3
SLOW, lacking spontaneity	Long delays before replying to some questions	2

RATING

DEPRESSED   His depression seems to be secondary to
                        his delusions   2

Formulation:

He left his previous jobs as an accountant and doing office work to take his far more demanding present job 'as a form of treatment for my introversion'. He is an introspective man who finds the interpersonal aspects of his work—which involves meeting people in many foreign countries—very demanding. During a previous trip he developed ideas that a colleague was going to murder him while out swimming with him one day. In his family history his father was an alcoholic who committed suicide after developing ideas that he was a homosexual. The patient himself has an unhappy marriage, and is unsure of his sexual orientation. All the above is the context of his present illness, which has the features of a paranoid psychosis.

Psychiatric diagnosis:

Paranoid psychosis
(ICD diagnosis: 298.3—acute paranoid reaction)
Overall severity rating: '4' marked psychiatric case

Extract from general practitioner's daybook:

Complaint: Depression
Diagnostic category: Entirely psychiatric
Psychiatric severity rating: '4' marked psychiatric case
GHQ Score: 42

Vignette of Case No. 210. An example of a marked psychiatric case (female)

Presenting complaint:

Mrs. J. J. was a 47-year-old housewife who came up to see if the doctor could help her to lose weight. Her scores on the present questionnaire and the depression scale of the Middlesex questionnaire had caused the GP to take a psychiatric history from her. Eighteen months ago she had come to London from the North and had never settled in here. A year before her father had died, and a few months afterwards her mother was found to have cancer. Nine months before she had had herpes zoster and had had post-herpetic neuralgia for some time after this. Some months ago she had felt very anxious, but more recently she had begun to feel that nothing worried her any more, 'because I no longer have any feelings, I have stopped going out, I feel that people are looking at me and talking about me behind my back, and everything seems such an effort now'. She had had a 'nervous breakdown' for 6 months at the age of 30 with weeping, dizziness and teichopsia which had been treated by her GP. Her present illness had started soon after her father's death. A recent exacerbating factor was that her unmarried adopted daughter had told her that she was pregnant.

Semistructured interview: RATING

Somatic symptoms: None   0
Fatigue: Occasional exhaustion during the day   2
Sleep disturbance: Loses at least 2 hrs/night despite hypnotics   2
Irritability: Occasional flare-ups over trivialities   2

RATING

Lack of concentration:	Constant, prevents reading newspaper or watching TV	3
Depression:	Episodes of depression, weeps, feels hopeless	2
Anxiety and worry:	Very distressed by constant worry over trivialities	4
Phobias:	Dislikes being alone, going out by herself	1
Obsessions, etc.:	Switches things off × 3, but no struggle, no distress	1
Depersonalization:	Has definitely had it recently, but not in past week	1

Manifest abnormalities at interview:

DEPRESSED	Moderate depression of clinically significant degree	3
ANXIOUS, tense	Many signs and symptoms of anxiety present	3
DEPRESSIVE THOUGHTS	Feels guilty, and inferior to others, is letting everyone down. Thinks all her feelings have left her	3
DELUSIONS, misinterpretations	Feels people laugh at her and make derogatory remarks behind her back about her People seem to be looking at her	2
SLOW, lacking spontaneity	Delays in answering questions, apathetic	2
FLATTENED	Depressive flattening of mood is evident	2
EXCESSIVE CONCERN WITH BODILY FUNCTIONS	Wonders whether high cholesterol in her blood will give her a heart attack (non-morbid rating)	1

Formulation:

The special features of her depression are her 'total lack of feeling' and her paranoid misinterpretations. Although she is now 'too numb for anything to matter any more' she still experiences a good deal of anxiety. She has well-held ideas of inferiority and guilt and disturbed sleep. There are many environmental precipitants of her illness, and these are listed above.

Psychiatric diagnosis:

Affective illness: depression
(ICD diagnosis: 296.2—manic-depressive psychosis; depressed type)
Overall severity rating: '4' marked psychiatric case

Extract from the general practitioner's daybook:

Complaint:	Obesity/depression
Diagnostic category:	Entirely psychiatric condition
Psychiatric severity rating:	'4' marked psychiatric case

GHQ Score: 55

ITEMS SELECTED FOR THE SHORTER VERSIONS OF THE QUESTIONNAIRE

ITEMS SELECTED FOR THE THREE 36-QUESTION QUESTIONNAIRES

'The 36 "Best" Items'

I	2	3	4	7	II	I2	I4	I5	I6	I7	20	2I	23	28	30	35	36
37	38	39	40	41	42	43	45	46	47	49	50	51	52	54	55	56	58

Balanced for 'Agreement Set'

I	2	7	I2	I4	I5	I6	I7	20	2I	26	27	28	30	3I	32	33	35
36	39	40	41	42	43	45	46	47	49	50	51	52	53	54	55	56	58

'Physical Illness' Items Removed

7	9	II	I4	I8	I9	20	2I	23	28	30	34	35	36	37	38	39	40
41	42	43	45	46	47	49	50	51	52	53	54	55	56	57	58	59	60

ITEMS SELECTED FOR THE 12-, 20- AND 30-ITEM QUESTIONNAIRES

(*Note:* The number before each item indicates its position in the 60-item questionnaire)

HAVE YOU RECENTLY:

7. — been able to concentrate on whatever you're doing?
14. — lost much sleep over worry?
35. — felt that you are playing a useful part in things?
36. — felt capable of making decisions about things?
39. — felt constantly under strain?
40. — felt that you couldn't overcome your difficulties?
42. — been able to enjoy your normal day-to-day activities?
46. — been able to face up to your problems?
49. — been feeling unhappy and depressed?
50. — been losing confidence in yourself?
51. — been thinking of yourself as a worthless person?
54. — been feeling reasonably happy, all things considered?
—*THESE ARE THE 12 BEST ITEMS*

21. — been managing to keep yourself busy and occupied?
26. — been getting out of the house as much as usual?
28. — been feeling on the whole you were doing things well?
30. — been satisfied with the way you've carried out your task?
43. — been taking things hard?
47. — found everything getting on top of you?
55. — been feeling nervous and strung up all the time?
58. — found at times you couldn't do anything because your nerves were too bad?
—*THESE ARE THE 20 BEST ITEMS*

HAVE YOU RECENTLY:

20. — been having restless, disturbed nights?
27. — been managing as well as most people would in your shoes?
31. — been able to feel warmth and affection for those near to you?
32. — been finding it easy to get on with other people?
33. — spent much time chatting with people?
41. — been finding life a struggle all the time?
45. — been getting scared or panicky for no good reason?
52. — felt that life is entirely hopeless?
53. — been feeling hopeful about your own future?
56. — felt that life isn't worth living?

—THESE ARE THE 30 BEST ITEMS

ITEMS SELECTED FOR THE 30-ITEM GHQ USED IN THE UNITED STATES

7 14 15 16 20 21 26 27 28 31 32 35 36 39 40 41 42 43 45
46 47 49 50 51 52 53 54 55 56 58

These are the '30 best' items, except that items 30 and 33 were withdrawn on the advice of American colleagues and replaced by items 15 and 16, since the former items were not easily understood by some respondents. Three further items had minor alterations to the wording to make them more comprehensible in the vernacular (original wording in parentheses).

HAVE YOU RECENTLY:

27. — been managing as well as most people would in your *place*? (shoes)
47. — found everything getting *too much for* you? (on top of)
55. — been feeling nervous and *hung-up* all the time? (strung-up)

NORMATIVE DATA SHOWING VARIATION IN GHQ SCORE BY SEX, RACE, AGE, SOCIAL CLASS AND MARITAL STATUS

SEX	60-ITEM GHQ—LONDON			30-ITEM GHQ—PHILADELPHIA		
	n	*mean*	*SD*	*n*	*mean*	*SD*
Males	203	7·73	9·78	297	3·42	4·89
Females	350	10·41	11·55	616	4·73	5·94

(t = 2·77, p < 0·01) (t = 3·28, p < 0·01)

RACE	30-ITEM GHQ—PHILADELPHIA		
	n	*mean*	*SD*
White	569	3·97	5·44
Black	339	4·92	5·96

(t = 2·46, p < 0·05)

AGE	60-ITEM GHQ—LONDON			30-ITEM GHQ—PHILADELPHIA		
	n	*mean*	*SD*	*n*	*mean*	*SD*
15–24	108	9·64	10·82	139	4·90	6·00
25–34	110	9·04	10·32	152	5·01	6·06
35–44	142	9·64	11·23	154	4·15	5·27
45–54	100	10·98	13·08	196	4·38	6·06
55–64	63	8·64	9·29	124	3·06	4·44
65–74	30	5·63	7·03	141	4·27	5·49

(Analysis of variance $F = 1·22$ on 5; 547 df. Not significant) (Analysis of variance $F = 2·00$ on 5; 900 df. Not significant)

MARITAL STATUS	60-ITEM GHQ—LONDON			30-ITEM GHQ—PHILADELPHIA		
	n	*mean*	*SD*	*n*	*mean*	*SD*
Single	(9)	(8·67)	(10·47)	175	4·73[f]	5·75
Engaged	21	14·10	10·45			
Married	103	14·20	13·20	561	3·93[c]	5·40
Separated	25	17·80[a]	11·80	56	6·82[d]	6·89
Divorced				29	5·31	6·23
Widowed	52	11·58[b]	11·40	81	3·88[e]	5·59

(Between a and b; $t = 2·06$, $p < 0·05$
,, c and d; $t = 3·66$, $p < 0·01$
,, d and e; $t = 3·00$, $p < 0·01$
,, e and f; $t = 2·42$, $p < 0·05$)

APPENDIX 7

SOCIAL INDEX (HOLLINGSHEAD AND REDLICH)	30-ITEM GHQ—PHILADELPHIA		
	n	mean	SD
11–19	111	3·65	4·69
22–9	94	3·42	4·47
30–7	71	3·42	4·18
40–9	162	3·83	5·85
50–9	188	4·52	5·81
61–9	120	4·93	6·07
70–8	93	6·00	6·26

(Analysis of variance $F = 2\cdot91$ on 6; 832 df, $p < 0\cdot01$)

NOTE: Hollingshead and Redlich's social index takes into account the head of the household's occupation and head of the household's education. A professional man with a university education would be coded 11, and an unskilled labourer who left school before the 7th grade would be coded 77. In the present data unemployed patients on public assistance have been coded 78.

SOCIAL CLASS (REGISTRAR GENERAL)	60-ITEM GHQ—LONDON		
	n	mean	SD
I	9	(8·67)	(10·47)
II	103	14·20	13·20
III non-manual	52	11·58	11·40
III manual	25	17·80	11·80
IV	21	14·10	10·45
V	3	(2·70)	(3·77)

(Analysis of variance $F = 1\cdot69$ on 5; 207 df, $p =$ not significant)

THE GENERAL HEALTH QUESTIONNAIRE
(60-ITEM VERSION)

Please read this carefully:

We should like to know if you have had any medical complaints, and how your health has been in general, *over the past few weeks*. Please answer ALL the questions on the following pages simply by underlining the answer which you think most nearly applies to you. Remember that we want to know about present and recent complaints, not those that you had in the past.

It is important that you try to answer ALL the questions.

Thank you very much for your co-operation.

HAVE YOU RECENTLY:

1. — *been feeling perfectly well and in good health?*	Better than usual	Same as usual	Worse than usual	Much worse than usual
2. — *been feeling in need of a good tonic?*	Not at all	No more than usual	Rather more than usual	Much more than usual
3. — *been feeling run-down and out of sorts?*	Not at all	No more than usual	Rather more than usual	Much more than usual
4. — *felt that you are ill?*	Not at all	No more than usual	Rather more than usual	Much more than usual
5. — *been getting any pains in your head?*	Not at all	No more than usual	Rather more than usual	Much more than usual
6. — *been getting a feeling of tightness or pressure in your head?*	Not at all	No more than usual	Rather more than usual	Much more than usual
7. — *been able to concentrate on whatever you're doing?*	Better than usual	Same as usual	Less than usual	Much less than usual
8. — *been afraid that you were going to collapse in a public place?*	Not at all	No more than usual	Rather more than usual	Much more than usual
9. — *been having hot or cold spells?*	Not at all	No more than usual	Rather more than usual	Much more than usual
10. — *been perspiring (sweating) a lot?*	Not at all	No more than usual	Rather more than usual	Much more than usual
11. — *found yourself waking early and unable to get back to sleep?*	Not at all	No more than usual	Rather more than usual	Much more than usual

HAVE YOU RECENTLY:

12. — *been getting up feel-ing your sleep hasn't refreshed you?*	Not at all	No more than usual	Rather more than usual	Much more than usual
13. — *been feeling too tired and exhausted even to eat?*	Not at all	No more than usual	Rather more than usual	Much more than usual
14. — *lost much sleep over worry?*	Not at all	No more than usual	Rather more than usual	Much more than usual
15. — *been feeling mentally alert and wide awake?*	Better than usual	Same as usual	Less alert than usual	Much less alert
16. — *been feeling full of energy?*	Better than usual	Same as usual	Less energy than usual	Much less energetic
17. — *had difficulty in getting off to sleep?*	Not at all	No more than usual	Rather more than usual	Much more than usual
18. — *had difficulty in staying asleep once you are off?*	Not at all	No more than usual	Rather more than usual	Much more than usual
19. — *been having frightening or unpleasant dreams?*	Not at all	No more than usual	Rather more than usual	Much more than usual
20. — *been having restless, disturbed nights?*	Not at all	No more than usual	Rather more than usual	Much more than usual
21. — *been managing to keep yourself busy and occupied?*	More so than usual	Same as usual	Rather less than usual	Much less than usual
22. — *been taking longer over the things you do?*	Quicker than usual	Same as usual	Longer than usual	Much longer than usual
23. — *tended to lose interest in your ordinary activities?*	Not at all	No more than usual	Rather more than usual	Much more than usual
24. — *been losing interest in your personal appearance?*	Not at all	No more than usual	Rather more than usual	Much more than usual
25. — *been taking less trouble with your clothes?*	More trouble than usual	About same as usual	Less trouble than usual	Much less trouble
26. — *been getting out of the house as much as usual?*	More than usual	Same as usual	Less than usual	Much less than usual
27. — *been managing as well as most people would in your shoes?*	Better than most	About the same	Rather less well	Much less well
28. — *felt on the whole you were doing things well?*	Better than usual	About the same	Less well than usual	Much less well

HAVE YOU RECENTLY:

29. — *been late getting to work, or getting started on your housework?*	Not at all	No later than usual	Rather later than usual	Much later than usual
30. — *been satisfied with the way you've carried out your task?*	More satisfied	About same as usual	Less satisfied than usual	Much less satisfied
31. — *been able to feel warmth and affec- tion for those near to you?*	Better than usual	About same as usual	Less well than usual	Much less well
32. — *been finding it easy to get on with other people?*	Better than usual	About same as usual	Less well than usual	Much less well
33. — *spent much time chatting with people?*	More time than usual	About same as usual	Less than usual	Much less than usual
34. — *kept feeling afraid to say anything to people in case you made a fool of yourself?*	Not at all	No more than usual	Rather more than usual	Much more than usual
35. — *felt that you are play- ing a useful part in things?*	More so than usual	Same as usual	Less useful than usual	Much less useful
36. — *felt capable of making decisions about things?*	More so than usual	Same as usual	Less so than usual	Much less capable
37. — *felt you're just not able to make a start on anything?*	Not at all	No more than usual	Rather more than usual	Much more than usual
38. — *felt yourself dread- ing everything that you have to do?*	Not at all	No more than usual	Rather more than usual	Much more than usual
39. — *felt constantly under strain?*	Not at all	No more than usual	Rather more than usual	Much more than usual
40. — *felt you couldn't overcome your difficulties?*	Not at all	No more than usual	Rather more than usual	Much more than usual
41. — *been finding life a struggle all the time?*	Not at all	No more than usual	Rather more than usual	Much more than usual
42. — *been able to enjoy your normal day- to-day activities?*	More so than usual	Same as usual	Less so than usual	Much less than usual
43. — *been taking things hard?*	Not at all	No more than usual	Rather more than usual	Much more than usual
44. — *been getting edgy and bad-tempered?*	Not at all	No more than usual	Rather more than usual	Much more than usual

HAVE YOU RECENTLY:

45. — *been getting scared or panicky for no good reason?*	Not at all	No more than usual	Rather more than usual	Much more than usual
46. — *been able to face up to your problems?*	More so than usual	Same as usual	Less able than usual	Much less able
47. — *found everything getting on top of you?*	Not at all	No more than usual	Rather more than usual	Much more than usual
48. — *had the feeling that people were looking at you?*	Not at all	No more than usual	Rather more than usual	Much more than usual
49. — *been feeling unhappy and depressed?*	Not at all	No more than usual	Rather more than usual	Much more than usual
50. — *been losing confidence in yourself?*	Not at all	No more than usual	Rather more than usual	Much more than usual
51. — *been thinking of yourself as a worthless person?*	Not at all	No more than usual	Rather more than usual	Much more than usual
52. — *felt that life is entirely hopeless?*	Not at all	No more than usual	Rather more than usual	Much more than usual
53. — *been feeling hopeful about your own future?*	More so than usual	About same as usual	Less so than usual	Much less hopeful
54. — *been feeling reasonably happy, all things considered?*	More so than usual	About same as usual	Less so than usual	Much less than usual
55. — *been feeling nervous and strung-up all the time?*	Not at all	No more than usual	Rather more than usual	Much more than usual
56. — *felt that life isn't worth living?*	Not at all	No more than usual	Rather more than usual	Much more than usual
57. — *thought of the possibility that you might make away with yourself?*	Definitely not	I don't think so	Has crossed my mind	Definitely have
58. — *found at times you couldn't do anything because your nerves were too bad?*	Not at all	No more than usual	Rather more than usual	Much more than usual
59. — *found yourself wishing you were dead and away from it all?*	Not at all	No more than usual	Rather more than usual	Much more than usual
60. — *found that the idea of taking your own life kept coming into your mind?*	Definitely not	I don't think so	Has crossed my mind	Definitely has

REFERENCES

ABRAHAMSON, J. H., TEREPOLSKY, L., BROOK, J. G., and KARK, S. L. (1965) Cornell Medical Index as a health measure in epidemiological studies. A test of the validity of a health questionnaire, *Brit. J. prev. soc. Med.*, **19**, 103–10.

ANASTASI, A. (1963) *Psychological Testing*, New York.

ARTHUR, A. (1955) *Delusions—A Theoretical, Methodological and Experimental Study*, unpublished Ph.D. thesis, London University, London.

BECK, A. T., WARD, C. H., MENDELSON, M., MOCK, J., and ERBAUGH, J. (1961) An inventory for measuring depression, *Arch. gen. Psychiat.*, **4**, 561–71.

BLUM, R. H. (1962) Case identification in psychiatric epidemiology: methods and problems, *Milbank Mem. Fd Quart.*, **40**, 253.

BOPP, J. (1955) *A Quantitative Statistical Analysis of Word Association in Schizophrenia*, unpublished D.M. thesis, University of Illinois, Chicago.

BREMER, J. (1951) Social psychiatric investigation of a small community in Northern Norway, *Acta psychiat. scand.*, Suppl. 62.

BRODMAN, K., ERDMAN, A. J., LORGE, I., WOLFF, G., and BROADBENT, T. H. (1949) The Cornell Medical Index: an adjunct to medical interview, *J. Amer. med. Ass.*, **140**, 530.

—— et al. (1952a) The Cornell Medical Index: III. Evaluation of medical disorders, *J. clin. Psychol.*, **8**, 119.

—— et al. (1952b) The Cornell Medical Index: IV. Recognition of emotional disorders in a general hospital, *J. clin. Psychol.*, **8**, 259.

—— ERDMAN, A. J., and WOLFF, H. G. (1956) *The Cornell Index Health Questionnaire Manual*, New York.

BROWN, A. C., and FRY, J. (1962) The Cornell Medical Index Health Questionnaire in the identification of neurotic patients in general practice, *J. psychosom. Res.*, **6**, 185–90.

BUSS, A. H. (1959) The effect of item style on social desirability and frequency of endorsement, *J. cons. Psychol.*, **23**, 510–13.

CARTWRIGHT, A. (1959) Some problems in the collection and analysis of morbidity data from sample surveys, *Milbank Mem. Fd Quart.*, **37**, 33–48.

CLOUSTON, T. S. (1911) *Unsoundness of Mind*, London.

COLE, N. J., BRANCH, C. H., and SHAW, O. M. (1957) Mental illness. A survey assessment of community rates, attitudes and adjustments, *Arch. Neurol. Psychiat.* (*Chic.*), **77**, 393.

COUCH, A., and KENISTON, K. (1960) Yea sayers and nay sayers: agreeing response set as a personality variable, *J. abnorm. soc. Psychol.*, **60**, 151–74.

CRONBACH, L. J. (1942) Studies of acquiescence as a factor in the true–false test, *J. educ. Psychol.*, **33**, 401–15.

—— (1949, 1960) *Essentials of Psychological Testing*, New York.

CROWN, S., and CRISP, A. H. (1966) A short clinical diagnostic self-rating scale for psycho-neurotic patients, *Brit. J. Psychiat.*, **112**, 917.

CROWNE, D., and MARLOW, D. (1964) *The Approval Motive*, New York.

CULPAN, R. H., DAVIES, B. M., and OPPENHEIM, A. N. (1960) Incidence of psychiatric illness among hospital out-patients, *Brit. med. J.*, **1**, 855.

EATON, J. W., and WEIL, R. J. (1955) *Culture and Mental Disorders*, Glencoe, Ill.

EDWARDS, A. L. (1953) The relationship between the judged desirability of a trait and the probability that the trait will be endorsed, *J. appl. Psychol.*, **37**, 90–3.

EDWARDS, A. L. (1957) *The Social Desirability Variable in Personality Assessment and Research*, New York.

—— (1967) The social desirability variable, in *Response Set in Personality Assessment*, ed. Berg, I., Chicago, Chs. 2 and 3.

ERDMAN, A. J. (1952) The Cornell Medical Index: V. Outpatients admitting department of a general hospital, *J. Amer. med. Ass.*, **149**, 550.

ESSEN-MÖLLER, E. (1956) Individual traits and morbidity in a Swedish rural population, *Acta psychiat. scand.*, Suppl. 100.

EYSENCK, H. J. (1947) *Dimensions of Personality*, London.

—— (1959) *Manual of the Maudsley Personality Inventory*, London.

FELIX, R. H., and BOWERS, R. V. (1948) Mental hygiene and socio-environmental factors, *Milbank Mem. Fd Quart.*, **26**, 127.

FOULDS, G. A. (1965) *Personality and Personal Illness*, London.

—— and HOPE, K. (1968) *Manual of the Symptom Sign Inventory (SSI)*, London.

FREMING, K. H. (1951) *The Expectation of Mental Infirmity in a Sample of the Danish Population*, London.

FRIED, M., and LINDEMANN, E. (1961) Socio-cultural factors in mental health and illness, *Amer. J. Orthopsychiat.*, **1**, 87.

GARDNER, E. A. (1968) Concepts of mental disorder. The relationship to criteria for case definition and methods of case detection, in *The Definition and Measurement of Mental Health*, ed. Sells, P., United States Department of Health, Education and Welfare, Washington, D.C.

GENERAL REGISTER OFFICE (1968) *A Glossary of Mental Disorders*, Studies on Medical and Population Subjects, No. 22, London, H.M.S.O.

GOLDBERG, D. P. (1970) Psychiatric illness in patients with diseases of the small intestine, *Gut*, **11**, 459.

—— and BLACKWELL, B. (1970) Psychiatric illness in a suburban general practice. A detailed study using a new method of case identification, *Brit. med. J.*, **2**, 439.

—— COOPER, B., EASTWOOD, M. R., KEDWARD, H. B., and SHEPHERD, M. (1970) A standardized psychiatric interview suitable for use in community surveys, *Brit. J. prev. soc. Med.*, **24**, 18.

GRUENBERG, E. M. (1954) Community conditions and psychoses of the elderly, *Amer. J. Psychiat.*, **110**, 888–96.

—— (1959) in Mental Health Research Unit (1959).

—— (1961) in Mental Health Research Unit (1961).

—— (1963) A review of mental health in the metropolis, *Milbank Mem. Fd Quart.*, **41**, 77.

GUILFORD, S. (1936) *Psychometric Methods*, New York.

GURIN, G., VEROFF, J., and FELD, S. (1960) *Americans View their Mental Health*, New York.

GUTTMAN, L. (1945) Quoted in Remmers, H. H. (1954).

HAGNELL, O. (1959) Neuroses and other nervous disturbances in a population, living in a rural area of Southern Sweden, investigated in 1947 and 1957, *Acta psychiat. scand.*, Suppl. 136, 214–19.

—— (1966) *A Prospective Study of the Incidence of Mental Disorder*, Stockholm.

—— (1968) A Swedish epidemiological study: The Lundby Project, *Soc. Psychiat.*, **3**, 75–7.

—— and LEIGHTON, D. (1969) Not available.

HAMILTON, M. (1959) The assessment of anxiety states by rating, *Brit. J. med. Psychol.*, **32**, 50.

—— (1960) A rating scale for depression, *J. Neurol. Neurosurg. Psychiat.*, **23**, 56.

HEIM, A. (1954) *The Appraisal of Intelligence*, London.

HELGASON, T. (1964) Epidemiology of mental disorders in Iceland, *Acta psychiat. scand.*, Suppl. 173.

HERST, E. R. (1965) *An Epidemiological Study of Psychiatric Morbidity in a Suburban General Practice*, unpublished M.D. thesis, London University, London.

HETZNECKER, W., GARDNER, E. A., ODOROFF, C. L., and TURNER, R. J. (1966) Field survey methods in psychiatry, *Arch. gen. Psychiat.*, **15**, 427.

HILDRETH, H. M. (1946) A battery of feeling and attitude scales for clinical use, *J. clin. Psychol.*, **2**, 214–21.

HOGBEN, L., and SIM, M. (1953) The self controlled and self recorded clinical trial for low grade morbidity, *Brit. J. prev. soc. Med.*, **7**, 163–79.

HORDER, J., and HORDER, E. (1954) Illness in general practice, *Practitioner*, **173**, 177–85.

HUMPHREY, M. (1967) Functional impairment in psychiatric out-patients, *Brit. J. Psychiat.*, **113**, 1141–51.

INGHAM, J. G. (1965) A method for observing symptoms and attitudes, *Brit. J. soc. clin. Psychol.*, **4**, 131.

—— (1966) Changes in MPI scores in neurotic patients—a 3-year follow-up, *Brit. J. Psychiat.*, **112**, 931.

INGRAM, J. (1961) Obsessional personality and anal erotic character, *J. ment. Sci.*, **107**, 1035.

JACKSON, D. (1967) Acquiescence response styles: problems of identification and control, in *Response Set in Personality Assessment*, ed. Berg, I., Chicago, Ch. 4.

JONES, A. D. (1962) *Mental Disorder in Anglesey*, unpublished M.D. thesis, Liverpool University, Liverpool.

KATZ, M., and LYERLY, S. (1963) Methods for measuring adjustment and behaviour in the community, *Psychol. Rep.*, **13**, 503.

KEDWARD, H. B. (1962) Social class habits of consulting, *Brit. J. prev. soc. Med.*, **16**, 147–52.

KELLNER, R. (1963) *Neurotic Ill Health in a General Practice on Deeside*, unpublished M.D. thesis, Liverpool University, Liverpool.

—— (1967) *The Assessment of Changes in the Symptoms of Neurotic Adults*, unpublished D.Phil. thesis, Liverpool University, Liverpool.

—— and SHEFFIELD, B. F. (1967) Symptom rating test scores in neurotics and normals, *Brit. J. Psychiat.*, **113**, 525–6.

—— —— (1968a) The use of self rating scales in a single patient multiple cross-over trial, *Brit. J. Psychiat.*, **114**, 193–6.

—— —— (1968b) *Abridged Manual of the Symptom Rating Test*, Liverpool University, Liverpool.

KENDELL, R. E., EVERITT, B., COOPER, J. R., SARTORIUS, N., and DAVID, M. E. (1968) The reliability of the 'Present State Examination', *Soc. Psychiat.*, **3**, 123–8.

—— and DISCIPIO, W. J. (1968) Eysenck Personality Inventory scores of patients with depressive illnesses, *Brit. J. Psychiat.*, **114**, 767–70.

KESSEL, N. (1960) The psychiatric morbidity in a London general practice, *Brit. J. prev. soc. Med.*, **14**, 16.

KINCANNON, J. C. (1968) Prediction of the Standard MMPI scale scores from 71 items: the Mini-Mult., *J. cons. Psychol.*, **32**, 319–25.

KLEMPERER, J. (1933) Zur Belastungsstatistik der Durchschnitts bevolkerung. Psychosenhäufigkeit unter 1000 stickproben massig ausgelesenen Probanden, *Z. ges. Neurol. Psychiat.*, **146**, 277.

KOOS, E. (1954) *The Health of Regionsville. What the People Thought and Did about It*, New York.

KREITMAN, N. (1961) The reliability of psychiatric diagnoses, *J. ment. Sci.*, **107**, 876.

LANGNER, T. S. (1962) A 22-item screening score of psychiatric symptoms indicating impairment, *J. Hlth hum. Behav.*, **3**, 269–76.

LANYON, R. I. (1970) Development and validation of a psychological screening inventory, *J. cons. Psychol.*, **35**, No. 1, Part 2, Monograph, 1–24.

LAWSON, A. (1966) *The Recognition of Mental Illness in London*, London.

LEIGHTON, A. H. (1959) *My name is Legion*, New York.

LEIGHTON, D. C., HARDING, J. S., MACKLIN, D. B., MACMILLAN, A. M., and LEIGHTON, A. H. (1963) *The Character of Danger*, New York.

LIN, T. Y. (1953) A study of the incidence of mental disorders in Chinese and other cultures, *Psychiatry*, **16**, 313–36.

LIPMAN, R. B., COVI, L., RICKELS, K., UHLENHUTH, E. H., and LAZAR, R. (1968) Selected measures of change in out-patient drug evaluation, in *Psychopharmacology—A Review of Progress 1957–1967*, ed. Efron, D. H., *et al.*, United States Public Health Service Publ. No. 1836, Washington, D.C., pp. 249–54.

LOGAN, W., and BROOKE, E. (1957) *The Survey of Sickness 1943–1952*, Studies on Medical and Population Subjects, No. 12, London, H.M.S.O.

LORR, M. (1960) Rating scales, behaviour inventories and drugs, in *Drugs and Behaviour*, Uhr, L., and Miller, J. G., New York, p. 519.

MACMILLAN, A. M. (1959) A survey technique for estimating the prevalence of psychoneurotic and related types of disorders in communities, in *Epidemiology of Mental Disorders*, ed. Pasamanick, B., American Association for the Advancement of Science, Publication No. 60, New York, p. 203.

MALZBERG, B. (1940) *Social and Biological Aspects of Mental Disease*, New York.

MANIS, J. G., BRAWER, M. J., HUNT, C. L., and KERCHER, L. C. (1963) Validating a mental health scale, *Amer. sociol. Rev.*, **28**, 108–16.

—— BRAWER, M. J., HUNT, C. L., and KERCHER, L. C. (1964) Estimating the prevalence of mental illness, *Amer. sociol. Rev.*, **28**, 84–9.

MARKS, I. M. (1965) *Patterns of Meaning in Psychiatric Patients*, Maudsley Monographs No. 13, London.

MECHANIC, D. (1962) The concept of illness behaviour, *J. chron. Dis.*, **15**, 189–94.

—— (1963) Religion, religiosity and illness behaviour: the special case of the Jews, *Hum. Org.*, **22**, 202–8.

—— (1968) *Medical Sociology: A Selective View*, New York.

—— and VOLKART, E. H. (1961) Stress, illness behaviour and the sick role, *Amer. sociol. Rev.*, **26**, 51–8.

MEEHL, H., and ROSEN, A. (1955) Antecedent probability and the efficiency of psychometric signs patterns or cutting score, *Psychol. Bull.*, Suppl. 2, 194–216.

MENTAL HEALTH RESEARCH UNIT (1959) A mental health survey of older people, *Psychiat. Quart.*, Suppl. 33, 45–99, 252–300.

—— (1961) *A Mental Health Survey of Older People*, Utica, N.Y.

METCALFE, H., and GOLDMAN, E. (1965) Validation of an inventory for measuring depression, *Brit. J. Psychiat.*, **111**, 240–2.

NEURINGER, C. (1963) I.Q. level and neuropsychiatric status on diversity of intensity of summantic differential ratings, *J. cons. Psychol.*, **27**, 280.

NORRIS, V. (1959) *Mental Illness in London*, Maudsley Monographs No. 6, London.

ØDEGAARD, Ø. (1946) A statistical investigation of the incidence of mental disorder in Norway, *Psychiat. Quart.*, **20**, 381–99.

—— (1952) The incidence of mental diseases as measured by census investigations versus admission statistics, *Psychiat. Quart.*, **26**, 212–49.

OVERALL, J., and GORHAM, D. (1962) A brief psychiatric rating scale, *Psych. Rep.*, **10**, 799–812.

PARLOFF, M. B., KELIMAN, H. C., and FRANK, J. D. (1954) Comfort, effectiveness and self-awareness as criteria of improvement in psychotherapy, *Amer. J. Psychiat.*, 111, 343.

PARSONS, T. (1959) Definitions of health and illness in the light of American values and social structure, in *Patients, Physicians and Illness*, ed. Jaco, G., Glencoe, Ill.

PASAMANICK, B., ROBERTS, D. W., LEMKAU, P. W., and KRUEGER, D. B. (1959) A survey of mental disease in an urban population: prevalence by race and income, in *Epidemiology of Mental Disorders*, ed. Pasamanick, B., American Association for the Advancement of Science, Publication No. 60, New York, p. 183.

PHILIP, A. F. (1969, 1971) Personal communication, May 1969 and April 1971.

PLUNKETT, R. J., and GORDON, J. E. (1960) *Epidemiology and Mental Illness*, New York.

POPOFF, L. (1969) A simple method for diagnosis of depression by the family physician, *Clin. Med.*, 24–9.

RAWNSLEY, K. (1966) Congruence of independent measures of psychiatric morbidity *J. psychosom. Res.*, 10, 84–93.

—— (1969) Personal communication.

RAY, I. (1873) *Contributions to Mental Pathology*, Boston.

REID, D. D. (1960) Epidemiological methods in the study of mental disorders, *Wld Hlth Org. Publ. Hlth Pap.*, No. 2.

REMMERS, H. H. (1954) *Introduction to Opinion and Attitude Measurement*, New York.

RICHMAN, A., SLADE, A. C., and GORDON, C. (1966) Symptom questionnaire validity in assessing need for psychiatrist's care, *Brit. J. Psychiat.*, 112, 549.

RICKELS, K., GOLDBERG, D., and HESBACHER, P. (1972) in preparation.

RORER, L. (1965) The great response style myth, *Psych. Bull.*, 63, 129.

ROSANOFF, A. J. (1927) Survey of the mental disorders in Nassau County, New York, July–October 1916, *Psychiat. Bull. (Houston)*, 109 (original not available in UK, quoted in Plunkett and Gordon, 1960).

ROTH, W. F., and LUTON, F. H. (1943) The mental health program in Tennessee, *Amer. J. Psychiat.*, 49, 662.

SASLOW, G., COUNTS, R., and DUBOIS, P. (1951) Evaluation of a new psychiatric screening test, *Psychosom. Med.*, 13, 242–53.

SAUNDERS, L. (1954) *Cultural Differences and Medical Care: The Case of the Spanish-speaking Peoples of the South West*, Russell Sage Foundation, New York.

SCHMIDT, H. O., and FONDA, C. P. (1956) The reliability of psychiatric diagnoses, *J. abnorm. soc. Psychol.*, 52, 262.

SCHWAB, J., BIALOW, M., CLEMMONS, R., MARTIN, P., and HOLZER, C. (1967) The Beck Depression Inventory with medical inpatients, *Acta psychiat. scand.*, 43, 255–66.

SHAPIRO, M. B. (1961) A method for measuring psychological changes specific to the individual psychiatric patients, *Brit. J. med. Psychol.*, 34, 151.

SHEPHERD, M., COOPER, B., BROWN, A. C., and KALTON, G. (1966) *Psychiatric Illness in General Practice*, London.

SPITZER, R., FLEISS, J., BURDOCK, E., and HARDESTY, A. (1964) The Mental Status Schedule: rationale, reliability and validity, *Comprehens. Psychiat.*, 5, 384–95.

SROLE, L., LANGNER, T. S., MICHAEL, S. T., OPLER, M. K., and RENNIE, T. A. C. (1962) *Mental Health in the Metropolis—the Midtown Manhattan Study*, Vol. I, New York.

SYLPH, J., KEDWARD, H. B., and EASTWOOD, M. R. (1969) Chronic neurotic patients in general practice, *J. roy. Coll. gen. Practit.*, 17, 162.

TAYLOR, S. (1954) *Good General Practice*, London.

TECCE, J. J., FRIEDMAN, S. B., and MASON, J. W. (1966) Anxiety, defensiveness and 17-hydroxycorticosteroid excretion, *J. nerv. ment. Dis.*, **141**, 549.

VECCHIO, T. J. (1966) Predictive value of a single diagnostic test in unselected populations, *New Engl. J. Med.*, **274**, 1171.

VEROFF, J., FELD, S., and GURIN, G. (1962) Dimensions of subjective adjustment, *J. abnorm. soc. Psychol.*, **64**, 192.

WALTON, D., and MATHER, M. (1962) Differential response to questionnaire items of neuroticism by 'defensive' and 'non-defensive' subjects, *J. ment. Sci.*, **108**, 501.

WILSON, J., and JUNGNER, G. (1968) Principles and practice of screening for disease, *Wld Hlth Org. Publ. Hlth Pap.*, No. 24.

WHITBY, L. G. (1968) Well-population screening, *Brit. J. hosp. Med.*, **1**, 79.

ZUBIN, J. (1970) Personal communication.

ZUNG, W. (1965*a*) A self-rating depression scale, *Arch. gen. Psychiat.*, **12**, 63.

—— (1965*b*) A self-rating depression scale in an outpatient clinic, *Arch. gen. Psychiat.*, **13**, 508.

INDEX